Twin Flame Romance

THE JOURNEY TO UNCONDITIONAL LOVE

Michelle S. Fondin

Los Angeles, California

Copyright © 2019 by Michelle S. Fondin.

All rights reserved. No part of this publication may be reproduced, distributed or transmitted in any form or by any means, including photocopying, recording, or other electronic or mechanical methods, without the prior written permission of the publisher, except in the case of brief quotations embodied in critical reviews and certain other noncommercial uses permitted by copyright law. For permission requests, write to the publisher, addressed "Attention: Permissions Coordinator," at the email address below.

Michelle S. Fondin, DBA
michellefondinauthor@gmail.com
www.fondinwellness.com

Publisher's Note: This work for entertainment purposes only. It is not intended to be professional health or medical advice. For actual mental or physical health advice, please seek out a licensed medical professional.

Ordering Information: Quantity sales. Special discounts are available on quantity purchases by corporations, associations, and others. For details, contact the "Special Sales Department" at the address above.

Twin Flame Romance/Fondin, Michelle S. -- 1st ed.
ISBN 978-1-0792941-5-6

Contents

PREFACE ....
1

INTRODUCTION ....
9

A New Age Dawning   11
Your Mirror   14
Union or Reunion?   15
Twin Flame Vocabulary   17
The Three Waves of Twin Flames   18
Feeling the Connection   19

1. SIGNS YOU'RE A TWIN FLAME ....
21

1. Instant Recognition   22
2. Attraction Even Though They're not Your Type. 22
3. Heart Chakra Activation   22
4. Intense Longing to Be with Them   24
5. At Least One or Two Huge Obstacles to Overcome   24
6. Mind Blowing Sex   24
7. Unexplainable Emotional Release   25
8. Immense Feelings of Unconditional Love   27
9. Increased Coincidences and Synchronicities   28
10. Angel Numbers and Signs Everywhere   30
11. Telepathic Communications   31
12. Increased Psychic Abilities 33
13. Intuitive Knowing That This Person Is Your Twin and That You're Meant to Be Together   35
14. Connection Gets More Intense Even in Separation   37

2. UNDERSTANDING THE TWIN FLAME CONNECTION..
39

The Origins   40
The Soul Contract   42
The Dynamics of Polarity   43
Finding Silence   44
Divine Masculine and Divine Feminine 47
The Twin Flame Problem with Polarity 49

Divine Feminines Rise to Shatter Paradigms   53

3. THE DIFFERENCES IN ROMANTIC RELATIONSHIPS .....
55

The Karmic Relationship   56
The Soul Mate Relationship   57
The Twin Flame Relationship   59
Must I Have a Twin Flame Connection?   65
Ditching the Labels   67
Merging into Oneness   69

4. STAGES OF A TWIN FLAME JOURNEY ....
71

Preparation   71
Activation   73
Elation   74
Irritation   75
Separation   76
Incubation   80
Metamorphosis   82
Reunion   86

5. STEWARDS OF LOVE ....
89

Defining Unconditional Love   90
The Elevation of Self-Love   92
Receiving All That You Are   93
Being Afraid of Unconditional Love   94
Giving and Receiving Unconditional Love   98

6. DIVINE MASCULINE, DIVINE FEMININE, DIVINE SEX? ....
105

Divine Feminine   108
Divine Masculine   111
Twin Flame Sex   115

7. THE WORK: HOW YOU TRANSFORM ....
121

The Layers of You   122
The Conditionality of Human Existence   124
Defining Human Conditionality   126
Embrace the Law of Karma   128
The World of Ego   130

Taming the Ego   132
The Journey Within   134

8. HOMEWORK FOR SPIRITUAL GROWTH
139

Homework #1: Take Care of Your Body   140
Homework #2: Meditate   141
Homework #3: Let Go of Control   144
Homework #4: Release Co-Dependent Relationships   146
Homework #5 Create Healthy Boundaries   149
Homework: #6 Move Toward Non-Judgment   152
Homework #7 Practice Gratitude   155
Homework #8: Moving Toward Inter-Dependency   156
Homework #9: Anchor the Light   158

9. THE LIBERATION OF SELF-LOVE
161

You Are a Co-Creator of Your Own Destiny   162
The Power of a Decision   164
Focus on Your Desired Outcome   166
Stay in Faith   167
The Return to Self-Love   168
Stop Waiting and Start Living   171

10. UNUSUAL SITUATIONS RESERVED FOR TWIN FLAMES
173

Connecting with Your Twin   174
Manifesting Desires Into Reality   176
Affirmations & Visualizations   176
Darker Forces Trying to Keep You and Your Twin Apart   178
Protect Your Twin and Yourself   181
Revisiting the Dark Night of the Soul   182
Raising the Collective Consciousness   183
Reunion with Your Twin Flame   185

Twin Flame Q & A
187

Glossary
193

About Michelle S. Fondin
195

Dedication

To my twin flame, my love, my heart, and my soul, I dedicate this work to you. I celebrate our journey and everything we've learned apart and continue to learn together. You are my everything. I love you unconditionally and will continue to love you every day in this life and beyond. For us, the poet Rumi has a special place in my heart and you know why. But here's a quote that expresses the integration of our souls:

The minute I heard my first love story—I started looking for you, not knowing how blind that was. Lovers don't finally meet somewhere—They're in each other all along. -Rumi

Love throughout the ages,

Michelle

Love is the bridge between you and everything.

—Rumi

PREFACE

*T*HE FIRST TIME I heard about twin flames, as an entire concept, was in the fall of 2018. I had already been on my spiritual journey as an active meditation, yoga, and Ayurvedic teacher for over ten years. I had been an Angel reader for over two and had vaguely heard the term twin flame as one who watches over you as you take turns incarnating here on Earth. My sister, who is also a twin flame, had been listening to videos and reading about twin flames a few months before me to clarify a push-pull relationship that made her feel a little crazy. So when I described to her what was going on at the end of November 2018, she said to me, "You might want to check out some videos. It sounds like you might be in a twin flame relationship."

It was late September 2018. I had just finished a huge cross-country move, prompted for the most part by my angels and guides. Moving to Southern California had been a lifelong dream of mine. But because of complicated family matters and also the fact that I owned a business in the Washington D.C. area, I was reticent to make the move when I did. However, being obedient to heavenly guidance, I packed up and relocated to Southern California with no home, no job, and not much of a plan. Thanks to my Angels I got a job, a beautiful apartment, and I also met my twin flame.

I wasn't looking to meet a love interest at all. Yet heaven had other plans. I was still in a long-term relationship with a man I adored, but who couldn't beat an addiction. With close to 3,000 miles between us, we decided to keep our relationship open just in case either one of us wanted to date.

When I met my twin flame I had no initial interest. I thought he was nice, but again, meeting someone wasn't my focus. Plus he wasn't my type. But by the second or third time I saw him, I felt drawn to him without knowing why. Often I would give him a flirtatious smile. Or at a meeting I would find that I needed to sit close to him. The first actual conversation we had was about marriage. He had mentioned he was looking to buy a condo and when I asked him where, he mentioned a few cities sighed and said, "But everything is so expensive here." And without thinking I responded, "Well, maybe when you get married, you and your wife can buy property together." He beamed and said, "You know what? I was thinking the exact same thing to myself this morning." In that moment everything changed. He got a gleam in his eyes and my first thought was, *Oh no! I didn't mean me!* But the look stayed and he shared more with me. Over the course of a few minutes we found out how much we had in common. The funny thing is before I said that, I had no idea whether he was already married, in a relationship, or single. *Something* told me to say those words to him. My words also revealed the first sign of twin flame telepathy. Without knowing it, I was reading the thoughts he had had earlier in the day and was feeding it back to him.

After that conversation I went home and asked my Angels, "What was that?" Immediately I got Angel cards and messages indicating marriage, dreams coming true, and a soulmate connection. Again my first reaction there was, *No! I'm in love with my boyfriend not this guy I just met.* So I asked again and my Angels reassured me that this guy, this new person, was the one I was supposed to be with and marry. I thought, *Surely there must be some mistake.*

But here's the thing, God never makes mistakes and Angels never lie. Almost immediately we started texting back and forth. Heavy flirtation followed. Then came phone calls and plans to see each other. It was an immediate attraction and an almost obsession leading to us coming together intimately. The first time I was so nervous because I hadn't been with any other guy in close to six years. But we clicked straight away. Being together was almost comforting and natural. The experience left us inebriated with the electric energy between us. As amazing as our time was, he pulled back. After our time together, he would text me daily, but his texts were more general with no flirtation whatsoever. I was confused because I know he felt our amazing connection too. When I called him on it he wouldn't explain it. For a couple of weeks we had the push-pull conversations of the runner/chaser concept you'll read about in subsequent chapters. Then one day out of the clear blue, we saw each other and the invisible energy between us was present once again. We only needed to look into each others' eyes and there is was. It was so strong that later that evening he insisted on seeing me. The time we spent was unmatched to anything I had ever experienced. The energetic pull felt surreal. It was as if we already knew each other. We didn't have an awkward feeling like lovers being together for the first time; but instead a rekindling of lovers coming home to each other. After that night I saw only him. I knew I loved him and without understanding it, I knew he was the only man for me. His one-word response to me after our night was, "Wow!"

    The next day, as magical and amazing as our experience was, he responded once again by texting dryly for the next couple of days. And yet again I blew up on him because I couldn't understand what he was doing. I was hurt and confused. Each time I would ask him why, he would respond, "It just gets too intense too fast."

PREFACE

My confusion intensified, as I would see him and he would have love in his eyes for me, but no follow through with flirtatious texts or invitations to meet up. Even so he would always text me every day several times per day. It was baffling. Finally about three weeks after our magnificent time together I gave him an ultimatum, "either commit and have a romantic relationship with me or tell me you don't want one but choose something." He chose no romance. My heart broke.

To the outsider it might seem like this guy was just a user. And in fact some girlfriends told me just that. But I *knew* it was different. He acted different. It was like he was confused about how strongly he felt so he just decided to walk away. Even after he told me "no romance," he continued to talk to me and look at me with interest and love in his eyes.

Feeling as if I might be going crazy, I told my sister everything. She explained what she knew about twin flame connections. The more she explained, the more it made sense. I then did my own research on the topic and all the pieces began to fall into place. Our journey is very typical of a twin flame connection. It's almost textbook and extremely strong. We shared telepathy immediately and it got stronger as time went on. The unfolding of the twin flame journey in this book comes through our experience.

What I share with you here is not based on scientific fact or hard-core evidence. As with anything spiritual you must feel into it. Everything I share with you is real and has actually happened to my twin flame and me or to others I know who are on this journey. This work is divinely guided and orchestrated by God and the Angels. As one who channels Angel messages I can assure you that I have infused the highest light and love of God in the process.

You will have your own experiences. Many of the examples I give mirror mine. But know that you are the only judge of your experiences. Through this journey you must learn to trust your own intuition. I'm not an expert, just a guide. I provide the map for you. The territory is comprised of your own experiences.

As the title indicates, this book is primarily on twin flame romantic relationships. My experience is a romantic one and the collective, I tend to channel, is in similar situations. In addition to my twin flame romance experience, I happen to be an Angel reader with a major focus on romance. During the course of this book, I'm going to be unapologetically blunt. My language may come out as brash or harsh. I don't normally speak that way in daily life, but my Angels and guides want me to make these messages crystal clear. This journey is not for the weak or faint-hearted. It's a real warrior mission that you were born into and one that is necessary for humanity.

You might be wondering, what makes me the romantic relationship expert. And the answer is, *absolutely nothing*. I'm not a relationship expert, nor do I pretend to be. In fact, I have a very good track record of many failed relationships. Counting only the relationships that lasted over a year in my lifetime, I've had in total five failed romantic relationships. I've been married once and engaged twice. I've been to numerous marriage and relationship seminars and read a countless number of relationship books. But like a professional boxer in a ring, I got right back up, learned to take the hits better and how to deliver a better punch (in a good way, lol). Having been a spiritual teacher for over eleven years, coupled with all of that relationship experience, the one thing I have is perspective. And as with all of my messages, I urge you to take what you need and discard the rest.

The one piece of advice I can share with you now before you delve into this book is to start journaling your twin flame experience if you haven't yet. Journal like there's no tomorrow. Here's why; twin flame romance makes no sense on the Earth plane most of the time. You will go through phases where you feel like you're 100% crazy. For example, your mind will try to tell you that everything you experience with your twin flame is a figment of your imagination. I can assure you now that nothing could be further from the truth. If your relationship fits the parameters of a twin flame connection, it's 100% real. But if you're journaling daily, you can go back and read what happened every single day leading up to the moment where you have those doubts. And those notes and journal entries will help restore your faith in the connection. If nothing else, it will give you a checkmark in the clean bill of mental health.

My Angels, in a channeled message from God to me about my twin flame, closed a letter with the following words that I now transmit to you, "Stay humble. Stay in faith. Be of good will. Be grateful." Good luck on your journey my friend, for your journey is ours. We are all one on this twin flame mission. Namasté.

Introduction

WHENEVER I'M ASKED THE definition of a twin flame relationship, I always answer, "It's a soulmate relationship on steroids." For those of us on this journey, even that definition can seem muting to the intensity of what we endure. For most of us, when we're ready spiritually to endure everything that the twin flame experience brings us, we've already been through quite a bit in the realm of romantic relationships.

It doesn't take a rocket scientist to see that the world is a mess. If you're able to look on a global scale objectively you can see that every aspect of life is suffering, from the environment, to animals and plant life, to political and social systems, and human life. Even with medical advances, disease is at an all-time high, especially lifestyle diseases. Addictions to alcohol, drugs, prescription pills, and other substances are skyrocketing like never before. Children and adults alike have electronic device addiction that is severely altering the human brain. People have become more isolated even though we have more means of communication. The earth is in need of major healing.

Now take the twin flame connection. Before they were even born, twin flames agreed to take on a difficult mission. They split their soul in two, incarnated into two separate bodies, agreed to integrate many lessons at high-speed intensity, and come together as humans to elevate collective consciousness.

The concept is not new. Jesus Christ came to earth as a baby incarnated as fully human and fully God, a twin soul in his own right. Jesus agreed to take on the world's suffering for the sake of humanity. He signed on to suffer in his human form and purge humanity of its sins, or separation from God. Since we don't have the power of Christ in one person, it's necessary that many of us in the collective awaken together to take on the task of helping to transform humanity.

I have heard many theories that the 144,000 souls, who are supposed to ascend to heaven according to the book of Revelations in the Bible, are the twin flame souls. I have also heard that the second coming of Christ is represented by the twin flame collective reaching Christ-consciousness together. No one truly knows the absolute truth when it comes to the twin flame journey. But one thing is for certain; twin flames are awakening and coming into union for a great purpose.

Introduction

A New Age Dawning

The question that remains is, "Why now?" I'm going to roughly outline some thoughts I have had surrounding this topic. It's not meant to be a scientific or historical study, but rather, thoughts to get the juices flowing and conversation started.

When I studied Vedanta in my studies of Ayurveda, yoga, and meditation, I learned about the Hindu philosophical principals of the *yugas*. The word *yuga* means a period of time of which there are four: *Satya yuga, Treta yuga, Dvapara yuga*, and *Kali yuga*. For the sake of this explanation, we'll focus on Kali yuga and Satya yuga. According to this philosophy we are now in Kali yuga or the age of darkness and destruction. These ancient texts claimed that during Kali yuga the average human lifespan would be about 100 years but would be ruled by disease, pollution of the environment, and immorality. According to the texts, by the end of Kali yuga human lifespan will be as low as 20 years. While the exact duration of each time period is disputed, we've been in Kali yuga since about 3102 BCE. Now let's go back to Satya yuga, the first of the four time periods. Satya yuga is known as the Golden Age, the age of truth and perfection. People were 100% kind and sin didn't exist. Humans didn't have to work and toil since the earth was rich and abundant. Religions didn't exist. One religion united everyone. If we were to look at the ancient Hindu system of time periods to explain the trajectory of human life, it would look bleak in this period. But what if we looked at it as a complete cycle. We are ending one cycle, Kali yuga and going back to the first one Satya yuga. It certainly seems that that's where we're heading.

Now let's take a more conventional example without getting too in depth. The book of Revelations in the Bible talks about destruction of the world and judgment day. It also speaks about the Earth and humans turning to sin, overindulgence, and selfish behaviors. Revelations explains that a split will exist between those who sin and those who repent and choose a more righteous and virtuous path. Are you starting to see a pattern here?

In New Age circles, people have been talking about the Age of Aquarius (our current period) as we're coming out of the Age of Pisces, which is said to have lasted around 2,000 years. Some say the Age of Aquarius started on November 11, 2011 or 11/11/11 (A twin flame number, by the way. :)) But even the exact date is debated and some say it won't begin for another 150 years. The Age of Aquarius is said to bring out the best and the worst in people, thus the division that is also explained in the Christian Bible.

One recurring theme seems to be present, however. We are in a transitional phase in humanity where things are not great and must somehow get better. Major change is inevitable. Those who accept the change and take on the challenge by standing on a higher moral

Introduction

ground on all levels will be the new rulers of the day. Those who choose to live in the same way, and continue to destroy themselves and the Earth as a result, will perish. It's as simple as that. Disease and addiction are just two examples of how humans are destroying themselves. Check out my book, *Enlightened Medicine Your Power to Get Well Now: An Integrative Approach to Healing the 7 Deadly Lifestyle Diseases*, to see some real but scary statistics on what's happening in humanity just on the basis of those two things.

Twin flames are awakening at lightening speed because of this shift and major change. We are the ones who have been chosen to lead the way into the direction of change. As a result of accepting this challenge, we are taking on the *sin* of the world just as Jesus did. But instead, we're doing it as a collective. Exaggerated incidences of human imperfections will show up in twin flames' lives so that these imperfections can be transmuted and transformed.

Accordingly, you will see some really bad behavior happening as you go through this journey. Addictions are common as are plain immoral behavior. Lying, deceit, betrayal, mistrust, pain and heartache are all being worked out on this twin flame trajectory. It's for this reason that I'm amused and baffled when I get YouTube viewers who *want* to meet a twin flame as if it's a prize on a dating show. My answer always is, "You've got to be kidding me!" This is not a fairy tale or kids' play. It's a painful and hardcore journey where all of us on it are asked to literally take up our cross and walk a heavy and heartbreaking journey to Calvary. The prize is resurrection and transcendence, but you must get there first and not all who try will make it.

Given these points, I don't know what you want to call this new era. It's a new age, time, and opportunity given to you and me. By understanding it better, you can live it well. You can try then to not get caught up in the process, but rather see the bigger picture. And the bigger picture is that under God's rule, all of us on the twin flame journey are collectively responsible for paving the way of this new era to get out of the destruction of our current one.

With this in mind, to start this process you must first understand who your twin flame is and how they fit into the bigger picture.

Your Mirror

You are your twin flame's mirror in many ways and they are yours. They can be your mirror by physical appearance. Many twin flames look alike and resemble actual biological twins. Your twin's background and childhood can mirror yours. For example, they might have had parents that divorced at age six and you did too. Your gifts and talents may mirror each other. You may both be musicians or physicians. My twin and I are both left-

Introduction

handed and we both like the same chocolate dessert. We are both introverts but also are very gregarious.

Mirroring also happens as you reflect back to each other your best and worst qualities as well as your childhood wounds. The intensity of the twin flame connection comes because of this mirroring. When you look into your twin's eyes, you are reflecting back to them everything that they are. In your eyes they see their deepest joys and greatest fears. As you hold up that mirror, they are forced to face their inadequacies and you are too. It's no wonder that running is one of the stages of a twin flame connection. Most of us would run from being faced with our darkest fears.

As you will see in the following chapters, that mirroring, which purges us from our darkness, is exactly what we need to heal and come back together with our twin.

Union or Reunion?

Oftentimes my YouTube viewers ask about whether or not meeting your twin flame is a union or reunion. In order to help you further understand, I'll use a parallel example.

If you believe that God exists and that he created you, he breathed his breath of life into you. And in doing so God gave you a piece of him. As such you are never separate from God. You only have the illusion that you're separate. Immersed in this illusion, we spend our whole lives believing that God is outside of us and we go on a spiritual search to find something real. Yet in reality we only need to look inside.

When we incarnated into human form, God gave us a part of himself and he also gave us our individual souls to carry out our life's work. In our individual souls God wrote our whole life. Some say that all of this is written in the Akashic records.

Thus, if we have established that we are always in union with God, even though our human minds tell us the contrary, it stands to reason that we are also in constant union with our twin flame soul. Since souls are boundless, spaceless, and timeless, the entirety of the soul exists in two parts in twin flame human bodies.

Try to capture this. All of the information necessary for this journey is contained in its entirety in every part of your personal soul that you share with your twin. Let's take this further. Every experience, hurt, joy, sorrow, and impression for both of you exists in you and your twin. You two are never apart because this information is constantly being recorded real-time. That's why twins will *know* things about each other without really knowing each other in the human form.

As a result, the more accurate term for a twin flame personal union is *reunion*. Since getting technical might be important to some, I will try to stick with the word *reunion* when focusing on the event that takes place after the runner/chaser separation phase. However, twin flame *union* will refer to the first time you meet your twin as a human form. That being said, I hope we can assume now that true twin flame souls are never separate just like you and God are never separate.

As frustrating as it can seem to keep things straight, let's attempt to focus on grasping concepts rather than getting stuck on vocabulary. Because once you can get the concept, the vocabulary won't matter as much. All things considered, let's go over a few key vocabulary terms that I'll be mentioning throughout the book.

Twin Flame Vocabulary

The twin flame journey comes with its own unique vocabulary. Many of theses terms are ones you haven't likely seen until you started to read or view videos on twin flames. I'll explain a few of these terms here. For further reference, please browse the glossary section at the back of the book.

The reason the twin flame connection warrants its own vocabulary is because of the upside down nature of how we come together. In traditional romantic partnerships, people come together through the physical first. For example, boy meets girl in person or online, they meet, talk, decide they like each other and meet again. They may eventually fall in love or part ways. Twin flames are together as souls first in heaven, then separate, but their souls have a homing device that calls out to their twin. Once they find each other, they recognize

the connection, connect, and then usually separate for a time. During this period of separation, much is taking place and many of their experiences are happening in the fifth dimension, or spiritual realm, which we will refer to as the 5D. When we speak of 3D, we're speaking of the physical realm, the here and now earthly plane.

The mention of divine masculine and divine feminine refer to the energies that people embody. Most often a man, of male gender, will embody the divine masculine and the divine feminine energy will show up in a woman. But this isn't always the case. In chapter six, we'll explain the dynamics of these two energies.

Other vocabulary that might seem more obscure to you will be defined in the glossary at the back of the book.

The Three Waves of Twin Flames

According to many twin flame stories, theories exist about the three waves of twin flame union. In my research, not everyone agrees about the exact timing and ages of these three waves, but they all seem to explain the reasons for each wave's awakening.

The first wave of twin flames, of which there were few, awakened around ten years ago or so. These twins tended to be born in the 1960s or 70s but again, the age or birthdate is not something agreed upon. They had many challenges but began breaking ground and paving the way for the second wave. The second wave started awakening around five to six years ago. They have had a ridiculous amount of challenges from separating and reuniting several times as well as a whole host of deep-seated problems such as addiction and infidelity. The second wave has worked out a lot of the karma for the third wave. The third wave of twin flames started to awaken around 2016. But the most recent wave started in about August 2018 with a huge awakening rolling out from October 2018 and into 2019. These twin flame couples are benefitting, in most part, by the work done in the collective by the two previous waves. They will have a much easier time reuniting. Third wave separation will usually last less than a year. In addition, third wavers are in their 20s and 30s, but may be in relationships with twins who are in their 40s and early 50s. Many third wavers are already coming to the union awakened and nearly ready for complete reunion.

Feeling the Connection

Moving through the twin flame journey is about learning to feel the connection between the two of you. Throughout this book you will see me repeat several times, "You know your twin. Your twin lives inside of you." And they do. You can perhaps say that the twin flame journey requires as much faith as believing in God. Many events and circumstances will try and pull you away from the belief that the connection with your twin is real. I can't tell you how many times this hap-

pened for me. But each time I was taken back to him and my faith in our connection grew stronger each time.

Finally, as you go through the highs and lows of your twin flame connection, know that nothing and no one can ultimately keep you and your twin apart. In a true twin flame romantic relationship you are destined to be together. It's written in your DNA and etched in your soul. God orchestrates your reunion and his plan always wins in the end.

1

SIGNS YOU'RE A TWIN FLAME

*I*N MY YOUTUBE VIDEO entitled, *14 SIGNS YOU'VE MET YOUR TWIN FLAME* (https://www.youtube.com/watch?v=Nfq0Aw3RMTg&t=2s) I outlined the following signs. While this list is not comprehensive, it will give you a picture of what you may be experiencing. As you read this list, keep in mind that you're not going to check off every item on the list as it applies to your situation. But you'll probably find that if you're a twin flame and in a twin flame connection, a majority of the signs will apply. Furthermore, I will go into greater detail on every sign throughout the book so if there's one you don't grasp in this chapter, keep reading. Even though some of these signs may sound like a normal romantic

connection, twin flame romantic connections always have more of everything.

1. Instant Recognition

When you meet your twin flame you'll find that you *know* them. You're not sure why. The feeling of comfort is familiar and some describe it as a feeling of coming home. The moment I met my twin I felt like I needed to be near him. It made no sense. By just being in his presence I felt calm. I felt this protective energy around him and I craved it.

2. Attraction Even Though They're not Your Type.

In twin flame romance, the connection is meant to explode all of your prejudices, preconceived notions, and limiting beliefs. Attraction to a twin who doesn't fit your idea of what an ideal mate should look like is confusing to most of us. My twin is nothing like a man I would normally look for on a physical level. I mostly had one type I was attracted to and he wasn't it. Now regardless of any man in front of me, he's the only one I see. It's so strange.

3. Heart Chakra Activation

Normally when you meet a love interest your heart goes pitter-patter. When you meet your twin flame, your heart will literally pound out of your chest. The image that comes to mind is that of a cartoon character falling in love. Remember those 20th century cartoons where the character's heart would protrude forward upon seeing his love interest? That is exactly what it feels like. Most of the time you're not going to have any idea what's going on. You could even fall into panic thinking you're having a heart attack. The palpitations are that strong.

This sign is related to your hearts finding each other. It's a telltale twin flame romance sign. God programmed your hearts to beat fast and hard when you find each other so you can truly recognize that this is something special. Along with heart recognition, heart chakra healing has started for both of you. We all have heart wounds and this initial union is designed to start the healing process.

In the beginning it was uncanny how my heart would pound every time my twin was in front of me or was about to be. This initial activation lasted for a couple of months. I would say to myself, "Good God when is this going to stop?" And the frequent feeling did subside. But now the heart palpitations happen when he's thinking about me and our thoughts connect or if he's about to call or text me.

You will also get major heart palpitations when you're going through a spiritual *upgrade*, which we'll address later.

4. Intense Longing to Be with Them

Unfortunately for most of us on this journey, this is the point at which the obsession starts. You recognize that the connection is undeniable and intense. You start to crave their presence obsessively. Looking into their eyes gives you a high like you've never felt. It's amazing.

5. At Least One or Two Huge Obstacles to Overcome

The twin flame journey is not an easy one. As such, you will notice at least one if not more huge obstacles that you must overcome in order to be together. One is a huge age gap. For my twin and I, we have around a ten-year age gap with him being the younger one. Twins will find that their partner is married, in a relationship, or that there are major cultural, religious, or societal differences between them. While huge obstacles can happen in other romantic partnerships, obstacles are almost a must in a twin flame one. When clients come to me and say they have no obstacles whatsoever with their romantic partner, who they believe is their twin, I can almost unequivocally tell them it's not a twin flame connection. Because the nature of the twin flame union is about shattering paradigms and healing the collective, there is *always* something major to overcome.

6. Mind Blowing Sex

Twin flame intimacy is literally out of this world. You may say things like, "You're the best lover I've ever had," even though you only had sex with them one time. With a twin flame, you just *know* each other. You know each other's likes and dislikes and lovemaking just flows.

Sex for twin flames is an awakening of *kundalini* energy. If you're not familiar with the concept of kundalini, check out my book *Chakra Healing for Vibrant Energy* where I explain it and go into detail on the chakras.

And the sex doesn't stop there. Twin flames also experience telepathic sex in the fifth dimension. It is the wildest crazy ride you've ever known. I would never in a million years believe that something like that is real, but oh boy, is it real.

7. Unexplainable Emotional Release

Almost every bit of the twin flame journey is unconventional but the emotional release phase was by far the most bizarre for me. When I met my twin flame I was going through a lot of hardship in my life, to say the least. I had just moved to California and didn't know a single person. I was going through a custody battle to keep my son and I was starting a new job. I wasn't exactly in a position to meet a love interest. And yet there he was. On top of it all, as you will learn, after the initial phases of crazy intense love, came the separation. It was during the separation that the emotional release started.

For someone who hasn't been through it, the state you find yourself in is really difficult to describe. All of us have been in love at some point in our lives and have had our hearts broken. You might be able to take a walk down memory lane to your teenage years when that one person broke your heart. You felt devastated as if the world might end. The guttural crying that followed made you feel as if you might vomit out your insides. Then after a few days, or maybe after a few hours, poof, it's gone like it never happened.

The emotional release designed to heal your heart and your twin flame's heart is incredibly deep. It's healing on a cellular level of every heartache you've ever had in this lifetime and others. When my twin first ignored me or ghosted me, I wasn't sad, I was angry. I've grown enough in relationships to realize that I'm not going to "cry over spilt milk" so it wasn't a feeling of sadness or rejection. It was more of a reaction that said, "That jerk. He doesn't know what he's missing." I was also confused over it because nothing really happened. But after that initial separation, every time I thought about him or saw him I would get teary-eyed for no specific reason. It got so bad that if I saw him during the day I would have to hold it together until I got to my car and then the floodgates would open. The weirdest thing about the whole experience was that there wasn't any specific emotion tied to the crying. I was peachy one minute and the next I was crying like the world was ending, but on the inside I was fine. After a short time the crying became, "Oh, I love him so much!" I've also heard of other twin flames having had the exact same experiences.

But wait, it gets even better. Every time I would see a picture of him or even see his name written, I would burst out into tears. It had nothing to do with the fact that I missed him or that I was angry at him at that point, it was an emotional release coming completely out of left field and there's nothing you can do to get away from it.

The question, I often get from YouTube viewers, is, "How long does this crying phase last?" And my answer is, "As long as it takes." You might have lifetimes of trauma to overcome. Your twin is helping you release everything you need to and you're doing the same for them. For me it took about seven to eight months. As you're healing, the fits of crying come periodically and then they only happen once in a while.

Even though it feels as if you'll never get through it, you will, rest assured. It gets easier since you now know what it is. And unless you have a clinical diagnosis of depression or another psychological disorder, don't take medications to try and suppress it. Let it out and let if flow, it's necessary for your healing.

8. Immense Feelings of Unconditional Love

The outpouring of love you have for your twin is something you may have never experienced in your lifetime. Most of us have only experienced love with conditions.

In the chapter entitled, *Stewards of Love,* I'll dive deep into love and the transformations you'll encounter in a twin flame romantic relationship.

Your twin could be the most broken person on planet earth and you will feel immense love for them all the time. You'll experience normal human emotions with them that may not all be positive, but the underlying feeling is that of unconditional love.

I had children early in my adult life and I had made a pact, with myself and God, to love them no matter what. As a child I never felt unconditionally loved and I never wanted my children to live through the trauma of not feeling the love I so craved. For this reason, I've practiced unconditional love with my three children since they were in the womb. And it made a world of difference in parenting. While other parents complained of their kids being awful and unruly, I never really had any major issues with my children. So when it came to opening my heart to my twin flame, it was an easy transition. Of course I had negative feelings about him at times, especially during separation, but I always understood who he was as a person and loved him for it.

9. Increased Coincidences and Synchronicities

God and his Angels are going to do everything to get you and your twin together. Once you have initial contact, strange occurrences will keep happening to put you and your twin in the same space.

The place where I met my twin flame wasn't even a place where I intended to be. A few months prior to meeting him I was living close to 3,000 miles away. We didn't meet under ideal circumstances. Yet, many synchronistic events brought us in the same time and place.

Even horrible circumstances will bring you and your twin together. I can laugh now at the drama that caused my twin and I to talk together. It wasn't very funny at the time, but even then I *knew* that God's plan was causing the drama to happen so we were forced to talk.

God will also synchronize events so other people talk to you about your twin or have them talk to your twin about you. When we had a separation after our first date together, where he got scared and ran, a random person came up to me and started talking about my twin. In my head I was saying, *Is this the same person as my twin that he's talking about? And why in the world is he randomly talking to me about my twin.* Of course at that time I had no idea whatsoever about twin flames or that he was mine. But the guy mentioned my twin's name and was saying all good things about him. I felt like God handpicked this person, dropped him into my physical space, and was telling me, "See, this is a good guy. Give him a chance." In every other relationship I've had that has *never* happened. It was always me convincing others that the person I was with was a *good guy*. (Well, that tells you a little bit about the caliber of men I would choose.) My twin told me this also happened to him. He said there was a person who had talked to me briefly and then went on for hours about what a great person I was to my twin. Mind you, this raving fan knew me for all of about five minutes. What in the world is that? That was God's hand showing my twin I was a person he could trust.

10. Angel Numbers and Signs Everywhere

At the time I met my twin I was seeing Angel numbers for quite some time. If you're not aware, Angel numbers are for example, 444, 777, 333, 1111, or seeing the same number three or more times in one day. Your Angels and guides will try to communicate with you in any way they possibly can. And if they can get you to notice numbers, they can get you to notice other signs they're sending your way. My favorite book to help interpret Angel numbers is *Angel Numbers 101* by Doreen Virtue. It's out of print but you can probably get a copy used.

When I met my twin, I kept thinking he was 44-years-old. I had no idea how old he was so forty-four seemed pretty close. It wasn't until about six weeks later that I learned his real age, younger than forty-four. The number forty-four is a twin flame number and also a number meaning you're surrounded by Angels. This was my Angels way of telling me, "It's him! He's the one. Pay attention!"

Besides seeing repetitive series' of numbers, you'll also see other signs like feathers, license plates with meaning for you and your twin, road signs, advertisements, or any other way your Angels can point you in the direction of your twin or give you reassurance.

My twin doesn't have that common of a first or last name. One time I was salsa dancing and the only time I looked up at the TV screen playing sports above me I saw my twin's last name on the screen. Then one time when I was walking around town after seeing my twin, a bunch of drunk guys walked by and started shouting his first name out loud. I know for certain they weren't talking about him, but someone else, since the contexts were completely unrelated and so I knew my Angels were giving me signs of affirmation.

11. Telepathic Communications

Much of our communication is non-verbal even though we're not always aware. I've heard that almost 90% of all communication is non-verbal, though my kids would disagree. Telepathy is a non-verbal exchange of information. It's been documented that biological twins have telepathy. Women who live together or who are connected by strong bonds telepathically share information so that their menstrual cycles orchestrate.

You might say, "Michelle, that's ridiculous! That's not communication!" Oh, but it is. We only think of communication as happening through words or the mind.

But we communicate all the time through our bodies and cells. Our souls and energy fields communicate with each other. Have you ever walked into a room and gotten freaked out because it felt creepy? Your body and energy field were picking up on the energy in the room. Maybe something bad happened there. Whatever it was, something was communicated to you.

Twins have communicative capabilities on all levels. They can communicate in all dimensions and across time and space. You and your twin communicate in dreams. You are in constant communication with your twin's soul. And in the waking state you can communicate via the mind with your twin.

My twin and I communicate a lot when we look into each other's eyes. We lived through a period of time when we couldn't talk freely, so the fact that we got to see each other helped tremendously. Also, my twin communicated with me a lot in my dreams. He would answer direct questions and tell me things. The first time he told me he loved me was in a dream.

Now, it gets even better. As I mentioned, in the 5D you're always in union with your twin. But you may not be consciously aware of that, nor would you necessarily have access to communicate with your twin's soul. I had a trippy experience that then allowed me to talk to my twin's higher self. (Believe me, I don't do drugs or even drink alcohol, and this actually happened.)

It was March 20, 2019, the night of the full moon. At around 4 p.m. I was on a break and meditating. All of the sudden like a flash of lightening; I felt my twin merged with me. We were one and there was nothing that could separate us. For the first time in a long time I felt at peace. I felt that he was completely integrated with my being. It was the most beautiful feeling I've ever felt. When I walked out a few minutes later, I literally walked into him. It was funny because I saw him disgruntled about something, but all I could do was smile because of what I knew. To top it all off, no joke, I looked up in the sky (because it had been raining) and saw a rainbow. After that moment, I've been able to communicate freely with his higher self. And his higher self gives me answers and talks directly to me if I'm in a quiet meditative state. It has been a blissful experience because in separation I couldn't get direct answers from him, but his higher self would tell me things that later he confirmed in person to be true.

12. Increased Psychic Abilities

In this collective awakening around 2018 to 2019 and beyond, you're not going to meet your twin flame unless you're spiritually aware. Even if you were to meet your twin flame, you wouldn't recognize them. Thus it stands to reason that if you've met your twin, you have some psychic abilities that are starting to open up. Perhaps you may have already been clairvoyant or at least intuitive and never honed your gift.

As for me, I've been psychic my whole life. I would have never called it that though. I grew up with a strict catholic mother who would have thought me possessed by a demon if I had told her that. But I always had conversations with God and the Angels starting at about age four or five. I just didn't know that wasn't normal. To me it was completely normal. Then I started *seeing* things happening. Like I could predict future events without understanding how I was doing it. Mostly I attributed it to good luck. Still, I knew I had this focused power.

I had a very bad break-up at the end of 2012 and in 2013 I went to see a psychic on the recommendation of someone I knew. During the reading she told me that I would be doing tarot cards like her. I told her she was completely crazy. In 2015 I started doing readings for myself and upon getting a Hay House certification through Doreen Virtue and Radleigh Valentine, I started doing readings for others. It was only then that I accepted my gift.

Once I met my twin flame I started channeling without cards. I guess I had done that all along, but it got much stronger after we met. The funny thing is one day he told me that he was a little psychic. He told me this completely out of context to the conversation we were having. Plus he's just not the type to say something like that. I told him about my abilities too. Then on the way home it hit me. I thought, *Of course he's psychic! He's the other half of my soul. We're the same. There's no way he couldn't be!*

You will start to *know* things about your twin. You'll know what they're thinking or how they're feeling. Then it will extend to other people and situations. You'll know the people that are trying to keep you apart. This is important information to know because as you get closer to reunion, people will show up who will try to sabotage the relationship. Remember this is a spiritual battle, not a relationship one. God wants twin flames to be in union as he is unconditional love. The more that couples are joined in unconditional love and become a collective force; God can better implement his plan for the planet. However darker forces will try to keep twin flames from coming together. We'll address this in later chapters.

13. Intuitive Knowing That This Person Is Your Twin and That You're Meant to Be Together

I shared earlier that the moment I spoke to my twin about our personal stories I knew we would be married. It had nothing to do with attraction, infatuation, or wishful thinking. I just knew. And I know he knew too. Throughout our initial time together that sentiment was constantly reinforced. Yet on the surface it made no sense. We were in different stages and phases in our lives. He is much younger. I had already had and raised three kids. We were raised in different cultures. We had other obstacles in our path too. I could find an entire list of arguments as to why it wouldn't work while all along I had the nagging feeling that it would. Even in my darkest moments in separation when I thought he hated me, I knew he was mine.

My YouTube viewers and those who I read for often ask me if the person they met or are in a relationship with is their twin. Personally I can't give anyone that answer. You are the only one who knows. And if you don't trust you're intuition now, to survive this journey you will have to learn. Much of what we experience on the twin flame journey is felt through our intuition, if you can't trust that, you're in for a lot of confusion. If you're mistrusting your inner voice, you'll find yourself in and out of psychiatrist offices and you don't want to go there. Modern medicine knows nothing of spiritual journeys. It's kind of like asking your pastor for medical advice. Right?

Another reason why you must trust your intuition is that others will think you're crazy. If you share some of the twin flame experiences with family and friends they'll cart you off to the psych ward.

In the next chapter you'll discover how to access silence and a meditative state so you can strengthen your intuitive awareness.

14. Connection Gets More Intense Even in Separation

I'm sure you've heard the cheeky expression, "If you want to get over someone, get under someone else." Well, in a regular romantic relationship that might work, but not in a twin flame romance. In all seriousness, after a break up or divorce the pain will eventually go away. Everyone tends to move on and healing takes place.

One surefire way to detect a twin flame romance is that the more you are separated, the stronger the connection becomes. It's the weirdest thing ever. You keep thinking, *Oh I can get rid of them. I'll just go far away and stop thinking about them.* It doesn't work because your twin lives inside of you. Your connection resides in your soul. And you're not getting rid of your soul anytime soon. So, good luck with that.

The best thing you can do is to accept that your twin is here to stay, whether in the 3D or 5D. Then embrace the fact that you always have someone looking out for you besides God and the Angels.

To summarize, a twin flame romance is going to look a lot different than a traditional romantic relationship. You will have experiences you may have never had with others. Many things are going to be beyond your cognitive comprehension. But that doesn't make it less real. Take the signs for what they are and add in your own to complete your list. Notwithstanding, the best way to know if you are truly a twin flame is to follow your intuition as I emphasized. Meditate, pray on it, talk to God, and you'll get clarity when you're ready to receive it.

Understanding The Twin Flame Connection

MUCH OF WHAT HAPPENS in the twin flame online community is like the blind leading the blind. Those looking for clarity often can't find it as many conflicting points of view are present online. As I mentioned, my twin flame and I are pretty textbook as a twin flame couple. I believe one reason for this is so I could help bring clarity to twin flames around the world. And I take this on with great responsibility. I'm not going to pretend to know something when I don't and I'm not going to present something that I've never experienced as being real. To that end herein lies real life examples from my experiences and teachings to help you better grasp the twin flame experience.

The Origins

Many strive to comprehend the origins of the twin flame journey. Some indulge in ancient stories and lore to explain from whence we came. You might hear stories of other planets, times, and existences. In my explanation I choose to keep it simple. The first reason is that I don't know enough about these stories, such as Pleiadians, interplanetary travel and so forth, nor am I particularly interested. Secondly, I don't believe that it adds to the understanding of the real-life experiences we all face as twin flames. Thirdly, I believe that God is too expansive in power to let us see the entire picture. So my explanations of such stories would be a poor attempt at trying to find God's reasons for this. In truth, no one really knows the entire picture, nor can anyone claim to know. Finally, my explanations are from real-life experience in the dimensions of which I'm aware as well as the channeled messages I receive from heaven. So that brings me to the story I *do* know and believe.

Once upon a time as a soul, before you came to this earthly plane, you made a soul contract to come down to earth to complete a mission. But before you did, as a part of this contract, you were chosen to split your soul into two with one half of your soul embodying one human body and the other half of your soul pouring into

Understanding The Twin Flame Connection

another human body. For the sake of understanding the two halves of one soul, we will call one half, divine masculine, and the other half, divine feminine. Part of your soul contract, as a twin flame, is to find the other half of your soul as manifested into the human form on Earth.

Some believe that twin flame souls incarnate together several times before finding each other. Others claim that twin flames incarnate separately throughout several lifetimes. In addition, they take turns and helping each other from heaven during the other's incarnation until the last incarnation during which they come to Earth together. To embrace any of these beliefs, one must first accept reincarnation as a concept, which I've come to believe. During a meditation early in my twin flame journey, I did see a past life with my twin flame in which he looked very similar to the way he looks now. In this vision, we were a king and queen and very happily married. Therefore, I'm inclined to believe that twin flame souls do incarnate together more than once.

Where it gets interesting though is to see at which point the activation of the soul contract comes into play. If you do incarnate more than once with your twin, it's perhaps for practice until you're ready for the unfolding of what you're meant to do together. Think of it as rehearsal for the big show.

The Soul Contract

Every one of us comes to Earth with soul contracts whether you're a twin flame or not. These are lessons from the Divine that we must learn, actions we must correct, and projects we must complete during our stay here.

Your lessons are either passive or active and sometimes they're both. A passive lesson is one in which you are a catalyst for someone else's active lesson. An active lesson is often a trial you must go through. Actions are either paying for past actions gone wrong or accumulating something good to carry us forward. In the purest sense, it's the concept of *karma* or as we put it, "what goes around comes around." Projects are things we need to build such as relationships, careers, family life, inventions, social constructs, and so forth. These projects are what we call *dharma* or life purpose. In two of my other books, *The Wheel of Healing with Ayurveda* and *Chakra Healing for Vibrant Energy*, I write extensively about the concepts of *dharma* and *karma*.

The twin flame soul contract seems to embody all of the above. It's a perfect orchestration of everything we came here to learn and be. Twin flames must first find one another, come together, separate to find themselves, and then find each other again, and live out their life purpose together. In your twin flame soul contract you've already worked everything out. On the inside of your contract are the bodies you agreed take on, the families you were born into, the languages, cultures, socioeconomic status, birth year, level of education, and talents you wanted to have. All of the obstacles and triumphs and pathways to them were all figured out in advance. But here is the kicker of soul contracts; when you are born, you forget. So when we arrive here, we fight our way through life until we remember. The twin flame journey is about remembering our soul-contract together, the one that we forged as twin souls before we came. And in the remembering, we stop fighting and start flowing.

The Dynamics of Polarity

We come to this earth from the space of infinite perfection. As we arrive we are immediately immersed into a world of duality. The first duality is that we are in a human body separate from the other. Then we are a soul and a body seemingly separate from our source. And the list continues from there. Everything on earth has its opposite, day and night, light and dark, pain and pleasure. We teeter back and forth from one duality to the next like a little silver ball in one of those old pinball machines propelled to and fro. In all of this division, we have a hard time finding oneness, though we crave it.

Many of us, in the course of our lives, seek oneness through the instant gratification of addiction. We eat, drink, gamble, and have sex into oneness. For others, we chase religious experiences, dogma, and rules as if God were outside of us. Some seek passion projects such as politics or causes to try and find unity. And the rest isolate themselves in lack of hope to ever find that oneness again and suffer in silence through anxiety and depression.

The problem in seeking oneness from an earthly source is that the very nature of an earthly existence is duality. Therefore, seeking oneness in duality is going to give you, well, duality. Then you're left wondering why duality is still happening even though you've done everything in your power to obtain oneness. Do you see the insanity in that?

The true way to oneness is from within. You're never going to find it in anything outside of you. Now comes the question, "How do I obtain access to the oneness?" And the answer is simple but twofold. The first answer is you already have. When you are awestruck by a sunset, the smile of a baby, lovemaking, or a peak moment in your life when you felt nothing could go wrong, you had it. The second answer is to experience oneness voluntarily; you must slow down the mind with regular periods of silence.

Finding Silence

In many of my other books, I speak about the methodology behind meditation and present moment awareness. For now, I will simplify the description to get you started. If you've never meditated or rarely meditate, you don't need any fancy audio tracks, videos, or objects. All you need is you and silence. Don't be fooled into others who say you need this or that. What you may need somewhere down the road is an experienced meditation teacher to guide you for some structure, but other than that you have it within you.

Today we live in a world infused with noise. We have every device under the sun to stay "connected." What this creates is a constant need to check our devices and remain in this electronic bubble instead of appreciating life directly in front of you. And even when you're not on your electronic device, others around you are. Unfortunately, many people are unaware that the noise they create with their devices, infringes upon the quiet space of those around them. All too frequently I've been trying to unplug in a public space when the person next to me finds the need to watch a YouTube video on high volume (well, that's okay if it's one of my videos, lol) or shout into a speaker phone while the whole world hears their private conversation. So the first tip on going inward is to find a quiet space. And if you can't, create one. I have ocean or rain sounds on my device with headphones so I can use that to unplug (ironic, right?). But most of the time I find a space in my home, car, or in nature to get quiet. Then close your eyes and allow yourself to be in the quiet.

In the beginning your mind will start to go crazy with thoughts. Don't do anything with them. Let those thoughts flow like images on a movie screen. Sit with whatever comes up. If it gets uncomfortable, that's okay. There is nothing wrong with sitting with discomfort. In fact it's healthy. That's your emotional body clearing. Up until now you may have been suppressing some emotions and your emotional body is saying, "Yay! Now it's my time to speak up!" When I worked with Dr. Deepak Chopra, and I'm paraphrasing here, he used to say about meditation, "If Jesus appears to you during your meditation, go back to the mantra." In other words, meditating is about detached involvement in the experience. Watch the experience without getting caught up in it. And that brings you silence of the mind.

Silence, if you're not used to it, can be disconcerting. Feelings of panic or anxiety are normal. But I promise you if you stick with it you'll find a deep sense of inner peace, even if only for a moment. Get to know your higher self, which has the most direct line to God.

The question that often remains is, "How long do I stay in this silence?" The truthful answer is, "As long as it takes." But for the beginner, start with five to ten minutes per day. After a week, add a second session in the morning or evening. Build your way up to thirty minutes around sunrise and thirty minutes around sunset. Those are the ideal times to meditate. However, make it real for you. Fit in your meditations as you can to fit your lifestyle.

When you're ready, find a teacher to help deepen your practice. I teach meditation periodically and have started online classes through Zoom conferencing. Look out for posts on my YouTube channel or Instagram account about dates and times for upcoming meditation courses. (YouTube: https://www.youtube.com/c/MichelleFondinAuthor or Instagram @michellesfondin).

Divine Masculine and Divine Feminine

In order to comprehend the twin flame journey, it's essential to fully understand the polarities of the divine masculine and feminine. Like the *yin* and *yang* symbol, these are two forces of energy that are attracted to each other like two opposite ends of a magnet. When you have a magnet, it will adhere to another metal object with the opposite polarity even if you don't want it to. The same goes for divine masculine and feminine. Once you have found your *energetic* match and you have learned to fully live in the essence of your energy, the two will be pulled together like a magnet. Underline and highlight the following concept: *When you have met your energetic match as a twin flame and you have fully become your half in the energetic match, there is not a thing you can do to keep you and your twin flame apart.*

Herein lies the issue. Most of us in the initial stages of the twin flame romantic journey are learning how to embody our energetic half. And because we have lessons to learn, wounds to heal, karma to balance, and normal everyday stuff, we take time in fully becoming who we were meant to be.

Since it's all about energy, it doesn't matter if you reside in a feminine body or a masculine body. Most often more women will be divine feminine and more men will be divine masculine. But that's not always the case. What does matter is that once you identify which one creates the polarity between you and your twin that you open to it fully.

I'm assuming that if you're reading this, you're probably divine feminine. So let's start with a description of the divine masculine.

Masculine energy is yang energy. It's represented by fire or is solar in nature. The energy is forward moving, penetrating, advancing, and pointing toward something. The masculine energy is going to go out there and get what he wants when he wants it. Again let's not get fixated on pronouns. But for the sake of simplicity, we're going to stick to gender specific pronouns for these examples. The masculine is the warrior, goal setter, and leader. He's going to make it happen.

Feminine energy is yin energy. It's passive, lunar, attracting, cool, calm, and collected. The feminine energy is represented by the element of water, which is responsible for cohesiveness. The feminine is receiving, open, and receptive. By virtue of this pure energy, it's strong. Have you ever had an object get attached to a magnet that you didn't want attached? The divine feminine energy becomes that strong when its power is focused and concentrated.

The Twin Flame Problem with Polarity

Have you ever tried to bring together two magnets with the same polarities? They repel each other don't they? As a kid I remember spending a countless number of hours trying to get two magnets to stick, on the ends that were not opposites, and no matter how hard I tried it never worked.

The twin flame connection is so incredibly strong that for the two halves of the soul to "stick", each person must represent one end of the polarity dynamic. Once the two twin flames are together in perfect union in the 3D, you'll often see them portraying aspects of both energies or switching between them.

Herein lies the problem and is the reason why twin flame couples are having so much trouble in this lifetime. Please bear with me throughout this explanation, as it may sound outdated, ancient, or sexist. But try to follow the logic as it applies to energy and polarity. Social norms as of 2019 have pushed men and women outside of their natural propensities for being. For example, women are pushed to take on roles that put them in *yang* energy in addition to *yin* energy. Oftentimes, they bear children, raise them, and also get a higher education, compete for a good position in the workplace, and have to go home and cook, take the kids to activities, mind the homework, and be a sexy wife or girlfriend. And men, have taken on more *yin* roles in addition to having *yang* energy. Men might be stay-at-home dads, or be at the workplace and then be in charge of picking up additional nurturing duties like giving the kids a bath and nursing them back to health when sick. Let me emphasize; there is nothing wrong with any of this. I will say it again. *There is nothing wrong with men and women sharing the work that was traditionally assigned to one gender or another.* However, when it comes to twin flame romance and togetherness, understanding how to stay in your energy *is* an issue.

Above I mentioned that the divine feminine energy is strong, like a powerful super magnet. Now let's take the woman who is nurturing at home and aggressive in the workplace. If she is indeed a divine feminine energy, she doesn't have to be aggressive in the workplace because her power lies in not being aggressive. She can accomplish more by being the energy of attraction that she already embodies. The only thing is she doesn't know this because modern society has not taught her. So she is acting or moving into *yang* energy in the workplace, in all likelihood, because she's seen men and women in the workplace act in this manner. To continue this example, if you're a woman twin flame, who is a divine feminine, and you have always acted in masculine energy in the workplace, you have some work to do. The reason is because that energy has likely spilled over into other areas of your life as well.

Now let's go back to the example of the same sides of the magnets repelling. Imagine if the man, the divine masculine, and the woman, divine feminine, are both embodying in equal measure both energies. What's going to happen? Are they going to attract or repel? The answer is, of course they're going to push away from each other. In addition, this is the case if one twin flame, let's say the divine feminine, is holding onto both energies but the twin flame divine masculine is staying in his energy. The couple will still repel because there isn't a perfect energy match to fit the pieces together.

Here is the sticky wicket. In modern society we get caught up in social issues and movements that will prevent us as twin flames in being in synchronistic harmony. Remember these are *social* constructs and not reality as it stands for twin flames. Purporting that a man can be more feminine or push a baby stroller has absolutely nothing to do with the energy dynamic. From the outside, especially if you're a heterosexual couple with energy matching your gender, it can seem that God is somehow asking you to go back to ancient times before women's rights and gender equality. In reality, if you're truly looking at this from an *energetic perspective* and not a societal one, it will make a lot more sense.

Let me give you an example. I have an acquaintance whom I've known for quite some time. He is married to a woman about a decade younger than him. When you look at him, you see he's a nice guy. He's calm, reflective, and kind. At first glance you can see that he might have a slightly more feminine or nurturing side to him. But he's also very manly. However, as he talks about his wife you can see that she (please excuse my expression) wears the balls in the couple. He talks about how she budgets his money and tells him how much he can spend. He explains how she says, "If you do this or that, I'll leave you." In this dynamic you can clearly see that his wife is living in yang energy. But it's not a nice yang energy, it's an abusive one. Many times I've wanted to tell him, "You need to man up and get your balls back. Stand up to this woman!" As an abusive person, she has stolen his masculine energy. And he has given it up to her. If this were a healthy couple, he might still embody more feminine energy and she might embrace more of the masculine. But it would be a healthy balance. She would perhaps be the leader in the family but she would respect him for his work, opinions, and look at him as an equal partner even though he's the more nurturing one.

In 2019, society is trying to argue that gender and gender roles don't matter. But they actually do. We live in a dualistic world and dualism is the agreement we signed up for on our way to Earth. And it's only in accepting duality that we can transcend it and reach oneness.

Most of the twin flame journey is about, not only finding your own power in the half of your energetic match, but also about becoming the highest aspect of yourself in that power. In this collectivity the divine feminine is leading the way to this grand awakening through heart chakra energy.

Divine Feminines Rise to Shatter Paradigms

Throughout much of human history women have been perceived as the weaker sex. In movies women are seen as needing to be carried, protected, and saved. Portrayals of 1950s American sitcoms show women as being subservient to their working husbands and catering to their every need while ignoring their own needs. Women are seen as frivolous, gossiping, and catty. As a result of this misperception of the feminine, women have been abused and treated unjustly. The few women, who were shining examples of assertiveness in history, were often summed up to be more manly and criticized as such.

In the 21st century collective of the twin flame divine feminine, we are here to shatter these paradigms. We can stay in our feminine energy *and* be powerful. And we don't have to sell our bodies or our souls to attain it. We don't have to compete, be assertive, or bold. By virtue of simply remaining in our power, we are powerful. It's a radical concept. Wouldn't you agree? Yet as divine feminine twin flames, we were put on earth to attain this quiet power. In the end it will help us break through barriers never broken through and raise the consciousness of the world.

Since the twin flame dynamic is so different from other romantic relationships in many ways, another way to bring clarity is to look at twin flames in comparison to other relationships.

The Differences in Romantic Relationships

*T*WIN FLAME ROMANTIC RELATION-
SHIPS work differently than most on every level. As I previously mentioned, if someone were to look at the initial phases of connection they would think the twin flame relationship was seriously messed up. You can't look at it through the eyes of someone who's not spiritually awakened, because it makes no sense. That's the reason it's a good idea to keep most of your twin flame experiences to yourself or share with a spiritually aware person, but even then, with caution. The trajectory of the twin flame relationship, within the realm of all relationships, is the unfolding of the pathway into unconditional love. But in order

to fully grasp how this works, you must first analyze typical relationships and their inner workings.

The Karmic Relationship

During your lifetime most relationships you form will be karmic in nature. These relationships are designed to teach you something. In turn you also are teaching the other person something. Sometimes those lessons are an equal exchange. Other times it can seem like you're the only one learning the lessons or vice versa.

Most often family members come to us as karmic relationships. These are the ones that leave you scratching your head and wondering why in the world they're in your life. You know the ones I'm talking about. It's the controlling mother, the alcoholic father, the competitive sibling who seems to get all the breaks, or the needy grandfather to whom you feel indebted because he raised you.

A lot of romantic relationships also show up as karmic connections. This often happens when you seem to be dating the "same guy" or the "same girl" in a different person. You wonder, *Why am I always dating the same type of person?* The reason is because you have a karmic lesson to learn and haven't learned it yet. Therefore, God will give you opportunities to learn your lesson many times if that's what it takes. Once you learn the lessons you need, you'll graduate from that type of relationship and be able to move on to the next lesson.

Now the difference between romantic relationships and family member relationships is that you may be in a karmic relationship with certain family members that you don't want to walk away from. That's when your lesson is to transform your behavior and reactions so that you can live in peace with those members of your family.

The Soul Mate Relationship

Meeting a soulmate generally feels really good. Everything seems to meld seamlessly. Upon meeting a soulmate, you have a feeling you've met before and you probably have in another lifetime. Often soulmates are members of your soul family or soul group designed to help you get on your life path. When you meet a soulmate you can talk for hours, time flies, and you will find many commonalities. In a soulmate relationship you will see an element of a higher spiritual connection even if you're not spiritually aware. With this person you *know* something else exists between the two of you, but you're not able to put it into words. In the realm of soulmate connections, coincidences and synchronicities happen so that you feel almost immediately bonded to this person. In love relationships the feeling can be quite intense.

One of my greatest teachers in life and a strong soulmate relationship came from an unusual situation. When I was a senior in high school I met and befriended a young art teacher in the same school. We had an instant connection and an undeniable attraction to one another. For the first few months, before I turned eighteen, we were friends and as much as we tried not to connect or see each other, it was nearly impossible. Then once I turned eighteen, it was all over. We needed to be together. The love connection was too strong for both of us. It ended up being quite the scandal that didn't unfold until right before I graduated, so we dodged a few bullets. But we stayed together for about two and a half years. I say he was my greatest teacher because everything I'm doing now in life is directly related to what he taught me. He was vegetarian and it was at the age of eighteen that I became mostly vegetarian. We took our first yoga class together and he taught me how to meditate. He taught me about Zen Buddhism, mindfulness, and the power of being present. At the time much of his teachings went over my head because I was in my late teens and I wasn't ready to learn everything he taught me. At the same time, it set me up for what was to come in my life.

As beautiful as the relationship was, it wasn't without complications. Soulmate relationships are also designed to help us learn and grow. They will also bring up some of your deepest insecurities and childhood wounds. If you are indeed a twin flame, I like to equate a soulmate romantic relationship to a training camp for the real thing. He had some deep-seated issues he never wanted to address and I had deep self-esteem issues he brought out in me that would take me a couple of decades to work out.

The difference between soulmate and twin flame relationships is that soulmates can be romantic, platonic or familial relationships. In the teachings I receive, twin flame relationships are always romantic in nature.

The Twin Flame Relationship

As I have described in previous sections of this book, your twin flame lives inside of you. Many of my YouTube viewers ask if a certain person is their twin flame. The first way to tell is to go over the signs of a twin flame romantic relationship outlined in chapter one. If most of these signs apply to you and the person you're thinking might be your twin flame, then the relationship probably fits that description. But the most important determining factor is your own intuition that this person is a part of you.

Many twin flame couples will tell the following story in different variations but the overall gist is the same. Previously I mentioned that I was in a strong soul mate relationship prior to meeting my twin. We were extremely close to one another. In addition, we too have intuitive capabilities with each other such as telepathy or feeling the other person when we are tuned in. So on the surface it might have seemed that this person was my twin flame. Looking at the twin flame checklist, this soulmate and I probably filled about half of the twin flame signs. But when I met my twin flame, it was a whole different ballgame.

First of all, not knowing much about twin flames, the signs came to me automatically with my twin because I was experiencing everything realtime and with great intensity. It was almost as if I was hit by a Mac truck full on. Even though I was still completely in love with my soulmate, when I met my twin I wanted to have nothing to do with the other guy. To put it another way, it's like my twin held the exact key that fit my heart and this other man held a similar replica, but not an exact fit. In addition, every single part of my body, mind, emotions, soul, kept saying, "Yes, yes, yes!" when it came to my twin and my guard went up when it came to other guys approaching me. For me being a sensual person, who happens to love it when men give me attention, this was a strange new experience. By the same token, I felt completely defensive of my twin. For example if anyone dare say anything negative about him or insinuate anything less than positive, I felt anger well up inside of me like I needed to defend his honor. Once again, that signaled another difference from my past behavior. Since I had always picked men with at least one enormous flaw, such as an addiction, an abusive tendency, etc., my mode of operation was to complain to others about them. But not my twin, he is perfect in my eyes. The other resounding factor was that I knew, with every fiber of my being, that he was meant for me. I knew this pretty much from the beginning. Additionally I knew it almost to the point of feeling insane at times. I remember seeing him early on in our courting and saying in my mind to him, *Hello husband! You are so going to be my husband soon!* And this was when *nothing* on the outside even remotely indicated that he might be my husband some day.

Secondly, during our period of separation, many things happened to show me that he is part of me. We had a fairly long separation period of close to a year. Now even though I knew at 100% that we were destined to be together and that we would get married; I had to *live* my life. I knew this intuitively, but also I had the good fortune of having a wise twin flame mentor who reiterated this to me. Living my life meant that if I needed to date, I would date. If sex was a part of that, so be it. Early in our separation phase, my soulmate tried to come back to me a few times. The first time happened over the phone when he tried to have some sexy conversations with me. The weird internal reaction I had was a feeling that I was cheating on my twin flame. Next, my soulmate traveled across the country for a visit a couple months later. Again, he tried to rekindle things with me. I let the rekindling happen because I wanted to see if feelings were still there. During the visit come crazy things happened. First of all, when my soulmate and I were intimate, it was fun but I didn't have any feelings for him. It was like I had a protective barrier around me. Next, my soulmate and my twin flame accidentally met twice. Finally, when it was time for my soulmate to take a plane back to his hometown, my twin appeared in a dream and escorted my soulmate to the airport. Crazy right? The same thing happened again when I later dated someone else briefly. Once the guy got too close I pushed him away hard. I even surprised myself because I acted so differently. Normally being single means the sky is the limit. You can date if you want to or find another relationship. But everything in me was ultra-protective of my twin.

Lastly, my twin knew things about me that no one else could know without me telling him. Through his intuition he would make comments that reflected aspects of my personality that no one else, even having known me for decades, had picked up on. For example, my twin was helping me troubleshoot a problem with someone and upon hearing the story, he asked me to look into his eyes and then he said, "Michelle, this is not you. The way you're acting in this situation doesn't reflect who you are." Now on the surface that might seem like good advice or a trivial statement coming from a good friend who knows you well. But the thing to remember is my twin didn't know me that well. The encounters we had had were minimal at best. The way he gazed into my soul and pulled out that statement was based on something he intuitively felt and knew about me and not on any direct experience or thing I had told him. Furthermore, when I would talk to my twin in the 5D, I would write or say things to him that were specific and poignant. Then when I would see him in person he would mention what I wrote about, in my secret journal, or he would look at me and say, "Are you okay? Is there something you need to share with me?" It was uncanny. But the greatest indication that my twin is with me always is that, during separation, whenever I experienced any bit of doubt in our connection, he would 100% of the time come to me in a dream to reassure me.

Most twin flames will almost "fight to the death" to prove to others that they're meant to be with their twin. In the early days of twin flame connections, when almost no one knew about it, I'm sure many twins were committed to lifelong sessions with psychiatrists, because it sounds completely pathological. And even today if you were to tell others about your twin flame experiences they might think you're nuts. They might want to cart you off to the psych ward if you tell them you *know* you'll be with your twin even if they're younger, older, married, or miles away,

In the beginning I had to cut off a friendship because I knew the nature of my twin flame relationship and that we were meant to be together. The reason is, this friend began advising me not to be with him and began to believe I was crazy or obsessed. She also constantly said, "I'm worried about you." While I understood the nature of the connection, she couldn't. For this reason I had to go with my inner gut feeling and let the friendship go. While you might be thinking that that is a silly reason for letting go of a friendship, let me remind you of the importance of the twin flame connection. We as twin flames are coming together for a much higher purpose. Along the journey into reunion you will often encounter naysayers and skeptics who will try and derail you from your purpose. Some will do it for the simple fact that they're not aware of this journey because they're not in it. Others are sent by darker forces designed to keep you and your twin apart. As a twin moving toward enlightenment, it's important for you to recognize when someone is saying or doing things to keep you and your twin in separation. Once you recognize this behavior, it's equally important to either let the person go or to keep information about you and your twin concealed. In the grand scheme of things, as more people are awakened and as they better understand the twin flame journey, much of the doubt will dissipate.

To recap, here are indications that your relationship is a twin flame one versus a karmic or soulmate relationship.

You feel that your twin "lives" inside of you. For example, you feel them at all times even when you're not consciously thinking about them.

You know, without a shadow of doubt, that the person you believe is your twin flame is meant for you at 100%. You will even go to great lengths to distance yourself from naysayers and skeptics.

Your twin is consistently sending you messages in the 5D and reassuring you of their presence in your life.

You feel protective and defensive of your twin as if you're defending a part of your own body.

The only thing that seems to make sense in life is that everything is pointing to the fact that you must be with this person. I describe it as a, "Yes, yes, yes!" feeling, but it could just be a sense of peace, harmony, and perfect fit when it comes to integrating your twin into your life.

Must I Have a Twin Flame Connection?

In the past year or so the concept of twin flames has risen to the top of blogs and videos. Like most trends people are itching to get on the bandwagon. Many are searching for the next big fad to help relieve them from the pain of living. That's why masses of people change diets often or join social movements. It's all a pursuance (unconscious most of the time) to find peace and happiness in something outside of themselves. As I tell most of my clients and viewers, the twin flame journey is not a fad. You are born with this mission and you can't simply adopt it. You're either a twin flame in this lifetime or you're not. When God decides to split your soul, it happens before incarnation. Additionally, God already has a plan for reunion with the person who holds the other half of your soul.

If you're uncertain as to whether or not you're a twin flame, I'd like you to ponder a few things. First, why would you want to be a twin flame? The journey is difficult and harrowing. Not everyone comes into this life with the inner strength and tenacity to be able to endure the battles that come before reunion.

Let's take for example someone who has the talent to be an Olympic swimmer. That Olympic swimmer, even with raw talent, has to commit to her sport even at a very young age. She has to give up playdates, birthday parties, dates, and many other things to practice her sport. Her parents have to invest a fortune in private coaches, swim gear, lessons, and travel to get to competitions. In order to win the gold, she must dedicate her entire life to winning. During the course of her career, her body suffers injuries and often she needs time to recover and has to take a medical break before delving back into competing. In addition, she must keep her mental state healthy. She has to deal with coaches who say she's not good enough and fellow competitors that may talk smack about her and her abilities. With all of this knowledge wouldn't you agree that not everyone is cut out to be an Olympic swimmer? I know I couldn't do it.

Now take the demands of the Olympic swimmer and apply it to a twin flame romantic relationship. The work is the equivalent of an Olympic athlete but in the relationship realm. Under these circumstances, do you now realize that it might not be all the flowers and fairytale romance you thought it might be? Whenever anyone tells me that they want a twin flame relationship, my answer is always, "Why?" It's the most painful and stressful experience ever. The rewards are great in the end. However, what you must go through is nothing less than torturous. During all of my relationship trials and tribulations, what I learned is that obedience to God is a must. Therefore, if you *are* a twin flame embrace it and surrender to God. But if you're not, appreciate and surrender to God in the relationships he has given to you.

Ditching the Labels

With all of this said, that still leaves the question, "How do I know if my relationship is a twin flame one if I'm still uncertain?" My answer to you is, "Why do the labels matter?"

Let me illustrate an example for you as to why labels are not important. Since the dawn of human history people have fought and killed over the concept of God. People have disputed over the name of God and whether he is called God, Yaweh, Allah, Shiva, etc. Millions of people have died over beliefs about God and his rules. None of the battles that have been lost or won change the nature of the essence of God. Throughout all of history, God has remained the same no matter what labels or rules man has attached to him. His essence is unchanging.

Whether you're in a karmic, soulmate, or twin flame relationship, the essence of your experience will be what it's meant to be. Your job as being human is to fully embrace and learn from whatever lessons God gives you. The meaning and purpose of what you endure must be absorbed in the present moment. And in that you will give full reverence to God and his plan. We attach labels to give some direction and cognitive understanding. But in the end, this is just a road map to help guide you. The fullness of relationship will come with your own experience and your perception of it. If you look to your experience with curiosity and gratitude, you'll extract the best out of the relationship. However, if you look to it with caution, skepticism, and analysis, you'll tend to see things more negatively and not appreciate the relationship for what it's meant to be.

If you find yourself stuck in the definition phase of your relationship journey, you're not in acceptance. In the end, it doesn't matter if your romantic relationship is a karmic, soulmate, or twin flame one. As you shift into the practice of unconditional love, you're going to bring light to all of your relationships. And bringing light to this planet is what you're designed to do. Otherwise you wouldn't be attracted to reading this book.

Merging into Oneness

The only benefit of differentiating anything is to then be able to merge into oneness of being. The path to enlightenment, which we all come to in the end, is to realize that we are one. Recognition of separation is what helps bring us to the immersive experience of wholeness. When you seek outside of yourself that which must be fulfilled first inside of you, you are constantly grasping. For example, you experience a break-up and instead of finding fulfillment inside of you, the impulse is to look for another relationship. The answers you seek toward oneness are never found in anything outside of yourself. It's this deep spiritual realization that your twin flame helps you recognize. Therefore, when a client or viewer asks me, "Should I go for this guy or the one I'm with?" I know where they are in their spiritual journey. If you are still grasping, you're not there yet. When the right person is in your life, you will know. And when you know, it won't matter if they are a karmic, soulmate, or twin flame relationship. The reason is you won't need the relationship to be anything specifically to define you and your life experience. Oneness will be yours whether you're in the relationship or not.

That being said, let's hop back to outlining the crazy twin flame journey to help you check in with what might be going on in your life. For example, I might want to drive to Sedona, Arizona to go on vacation, but if I don't have a GPS to guide me, knowing myself and

TWIN FLAME ROMANCE

my sense of direction, I *will* get lost along the way. All things considered, let's spend some time exploring how your journey to unconditional love and, therefore oneness, might unfold to help you get there without getting too lost.

4

Stages of a Twin Flame Journey

*T*HE FOLLOWING ARE AN example of the typical stages of the twin flame romance journey. Most twin flame couples will experiences all of these or a variation of most of them. Try not to worry too much if your journey is not exact. However, if you've been in a twin flame connection for more than a month or two, you will recognize most of these stages.

Preparation

Before you meet your twin flame, the universe is preparing you for your meeting. This can take decades or a few months. I believe that my whole life prepared me for the moment I met mine. Yet looking back, I can see that events started lining up about a year before we met. In the fall of 2017, I had a major breakdown in my romantic relationship. We had had some big problems before, but this one caused me to precipitate my plans to move to California. In December 2017, I took a trip to Anaheim, California (where I would eventually get a job) to start looking for places to live. Then problems with my ex-husband caused me to move one month earlier than I had planned. The job I ended up getting was only hiring for my position, the month I arrived. And, consequently, the job was in the same city where I met my twin. Upon moving I started going to a church that has a primarily Asian-American congregation. While I didn't meet my twin at church, he is part Asian. As you can see, God will put you at the right place at the right time for you to meet your twin flame. And he will heighten your awareness so you recognize them.

The preparation phase can also include the lessons you learn in other relationships. My last long-term relationship was with a man who was my soulmate. We were together for a little more than five years. We were very much in love and I loved him more than any man prior to meeting him. However, he suffered from alcohol and drug addiction and his addictions were a destructive force for both of us. As much as he tried to overcome the addictions, he couldn't. During the five years I was with him, I had enormous personal growth. I became a published author, writing and publishing seven books. I learned a lot about alcohol and drug addiction and was able to help his family learn. In addition, I was able to volunteer my time teaching yoga at a rehab center. And I became much closer to God. I loved him like crazy and gave him the love he so craved but never received. I also gave him the love he couldn't give himself. The strength and tenacity it took to be in that relationship prepared me for the difficulty of separation with my twin flame.

Activation

Activation is when your heart recognizes your twin. First, your soul recognizes them. That's why you'll have the feeling that you've known them before or you'll have a feeling of home. For me, it was an overwhelming sense of peace whenever he was around. I also mentioned I had a longing to be near him. At first it was pleasant but not a necessity. But when my heart recognized his, it was all over.

Your heart will activate in many ways. For example, your heart will beat very fast when they're near. These palpitations can seem worrisome in the beginning since you have no idea what's going on. You might think you have a heart murmur. With my twin, after our first in person conversation with each other, our hearts started to recognize each other. Then each time I saw him, my heart would nearly pound out of my chest. It was uncanny how this happened every single time. Sometimes I would feel faint when he was near.

Then the heart palpitations got more intense as I would think about him or when I could sense he was thinking about me. Once we reached integration, the conscious merging of our souls, I would feel the heart palpitations when he was reading a text or thinking about me in any way.

In the initial phases of activation, the heart chakra is becoming open to your twin's heart for the purpose of recognition and healing. We have wounds from our childhood, past experiences, and past lives. While you may have been working through hurt and sorrow throughout your life, this activation is designed to help you purge any remaining hurt your heart has held onto. Your twin is going through a similar process as well.

Elation

The elation stage occurs after the heart chakra activation. Elation can be compared to the honeymoon phase of a relationship where you feel completely connected and immersed with your twin. Elation can last anywhere from a day to several months. It is accompanied with great intensity. You might experience love at first sight. You might feel scared, excited, blown away, and floored all at the same time. You have a longing to be with them, look into their eyes, touch them, talk to them, and never let them go.

For my twin and I this stage, because of our circumstances, only lasted a few weeks. We had a few weeks of intense texting and wanting to see each other. Once we saw each other the intensity got stronger. Yet because of the intensity, we were not fully immersed in the experience. During the elation stage, we took turns "running" from each other. He would get intense with me and I would back off. Then I would get intense with him and he would. But in the end we both truly wanted to be with each other, we were just not prepared to handle the intensity of our feelings for one another. Often it's this twin flame intensity that leads to the irritation phase.

Irritation

You recognize almost immediately that this is a special relationship. Even without the cognizance of a twin flame romance, you *know* inside that this person is meant to be in your life. You feel insanely good when you're with them. But you also feel so bad. And you can't figure out why you feel bad. This person, with whom you share such great affinity, starts to trigger you in ways that other people have, but also triggers you in ways that you didn't know you could be triggered. It's a bizarre sensation.

My twin made me crazy. I had worked through a lot in my previous relationship. I had done a lot of internal and spiritual work. That relationship caused me to grow in ways I never thought possible. When I met my twin I thought I knew how to handle romantic relationships. I knew what to do and what not to do. I had book smarts, street smarts, and a strong spiritual background. Without doing much, my twin made me revert back to behavior I knew was wrong. I overreacted to the things he was doing or not doing. What's worse is that I had no idea why I was reacting in that way to him. He pushed buttons in me I didn't even know I had. I know I also pushed his buttons. And he didn't like it at all.

Remember, you are your twin's mirror and they are yours. They're going to hold up that mirror and show you the stuff you need to work on. Through them you're going to see every insecurity, fear, and wound you've ever had. Your gifts will be magnified and so will your shortcomings.

Usually what's happening at this time is that the fire is turned up high and sparks start to fly. The good feelings of the elation stage get overshadowed by the intensity of the irritation stage. At this point, one of the twins will start to run and the other will start to chase.

Separation

After the initial meeting and blissful phase of your twin flame union, comes the irritation due to mirroring, and then the separation phase. Twin flame separation is one of the most painful and necessary parts of the process.

Runner / Chaser

Because of the intensity of the connection, one twin is going to run. The one running is usually the divine masculine and the one chasing is typically the divine feminine. This is also referred to as the runner/ chaser dynamic. The divine feminine recognizes the soul connection and wants it more than ever, so she starts to chase it. The divine masculine seeing only the yang or chaser energy starts to run. Remember, both twins are also feeling the pain through mirroring. Being the one who's more spiritually aware, the feminine, is more apt to want to deal with the pain while still having her masculine twin. The masculine needs to go off in the corner and lick his wounds, so to speak. He wants to feel powerful, but he can't if his feminine is chasing him and also pointing out everything he's doing wrong. Also, in seeing all of his insecurities, shortcomings, and childhood wounds, he's in a space of deep vulnerability. He doesn't want to be with his feminine when he's feeling that vulnerable. He wants to gain his inner strength again before he can face her.

The one who is chasing must remain cognizant that the runner is running for a reason. Energetically, the twins are not matched when one is chasing, especially if it's the divine feminine. At times, both twins are running. This happened to my twin and me in the beginning. Afraid of being hurt, I "ran" from him by sending him texts that sounded panicky and threatening to run if he didn't answer me back. At one point, I even told him I was done because I didn't feel he was reaching out enough. He ran by being evasive, vague in texts, or by not calling me. We were both at fault. But in the end he was the runner. No. Let me qualify that, he was the ultimate sprinter. And boy oh boy nothing hurts more than knowing your soul is running from you.

It hurts on many levels because usually by the time your twin runs from you, you *know* you're soul connected, even if you don't have the vocabulary to pinpoint the word *twin flame*. You're hurting because your twin rejected you. This person, with whom you have great affinity, ran and you're wondering what *you* did wrong. You're hurting because of the sorrow of missing them. You're hurting because you remember what it's like to look into their eyes and see infinity. And you're hurting because you have no idea why they ran in the first place. It's an awful feeling to have your twin leave you and cuts deeper than any other separation. Yet, it's in this separation that your personal transformation can begin.

Stop the Chasing

The only way to get your twin to stop running is to stop chasing. For twin flames this is easier said than done. When dealing with two people, who are not soul connected to the intensity that twin flames are, it's a done deal. You stop texting, calling, and reaching out, the other person decides to reach out to you, and voilà it's done. But for twin flames, they see, feel, hear, and sense you on every level. Let's suppose you stop reaching out to them in the 3D. You put away your phone, social media, and other devices when it comes to your twin. You

Stages of a Twin Flame Journey

vow to give them their space and let them come to you. Well, you have to remember that you and your twin are connected in the 5D. Therefore, your twin *feels* your energy. Even if you've stopped all external signs of chasing, your twin will know if you're chasing internally.

At this point you're suffering. You're dying to hear from them. To put it bluntly, you're a basket case. You cry every time you think about them, hear their name, or see signs that remind you of them. When you're in this space of desperation, your twin feels it. *I know, it sucks big time.* I can feel your pain because I've been there and it lasted a long time.

During this phase you just want to send one little text to see how they'll react. But mind you, that is still chasing. What you want to do is reverse the energy. The moment you go into yang energy during this separation phase, your twin will continue to run.

Why Separation Must Occur

Separation has to happen between you and your twin because of the work you both have to do in order to come into reunion. Twin flames together are designed to do great spiritual work. And they can't do the level of spiritual work they need to do for the world unless they've worked out the kinks within themselves. Since twin flame souls equal a great magnitude of intensity, they will destroy each other if they're working through their respective baggage together. Remember you are connected to your twin for the good and bad. Some twins have crazy amounts of stuff they need to work through such as addictions, abusive marriages, custody battles, and other legal issues to give just a few examples. Normal people, who are not twin flames, can work through these things organically. And some couples make it and some don't. But it's too important to God and the universe that you two make it through on your own separately, so that God can guarantee your successful union together.

Incubation

During this period of separation, healing is taking place but you are just more shell-shocked than anything else. At this phase you may have hit what seems like depression. The incubation phase is also known as the *dark night of the soul*. You don't want to go out. You have no desire to date anyone else. You're still reeling from the feeling of having this wonderful person come into your life and then leave so suddenly. You don't understand the separation, why it's happening, and you're wondering if you will ever see your beloved again. You feel like you're going crazy. And there's no way you can share with anyone because you're certain they will think you're crazy too.

Incubation or *dark night of the soul* happens so that you can heal wounds from your past. You are recalibrating and clearing away energies you no longer need. And that takes work. In addition, you're working through karmic lessons and even past life karma. Furthermore, the healing is happening at lightening speed. Ultimately, that's why you feel so crappy for a concentrated amount of time.

Here's how I felt during incubation. I would go to work, try to get through the day while keeping it all together, and for me that wasn't easy because I had to "run into" my twin from time to time. Then at the end of the day, I would get into my car and usually burst into tears and cry all the way home (not knowing why) or get home and cry until I went to sleep. I would write him letters and poems (that I never gave to him). I would hear songs that spoke to me about him and our situation. And I couldn't stop thinking about him all the time.

Once I started to figure out that we were twin flames, I would watch spiritual videos, read blogs, and immerse myself in anything else to grow spiritually. But most of the time I was just too exhausted to deal with anything other than work and the obsession with my twin. I wanted to sit in silence most of the time. And I wanted to be absorbed in my thoughts about him because that was the only way I could feel connected to him. I longed to be with him so badly that it hurt every single day.

But even in the midst of this insanity, deep down you know you're sane. You know this is real. You have a conscious awareness that what you're experiencing is what you need to experience.

For me the most insane healing experience I had with my twin was staring at a picture of him every single day. Just looking at his picture would make me cry all the time for months. The day I could look at his picture and not cry was when I knew that I was starting to change and that healing was taking place. That was a sign of my own metamorphosis.

Metamorphosis

After incubation, whether it lasts a few weeks to several months or years, the metamorphosis phase will begin. The beauty of this stage is that your twin's higher self is actively helping you through this phase.

In this stage, strange things are happening daily. The incessant symptoms and signs are bringing you to higher states of consciousness. Your twin is also going through these symptoms but may not be fully aware. Sometimes they are called ascension symptoms. I'm going to list a few that I had and you may find that some resonate with you.

- Night waking around 2-3 a.m.
- Constant dreams about your twin flame either speaking to you or sending you messages.
- Hot flashes or a feeling of heat like someone is on top of you
- Heart palpitations
- Sexual arousal when you're not even thinking about sex

- Hair getting really dry and brittle or hair falling out
- A feeling of a presence, like your twin is right there with you
- Tingles or goosebumps on your arms or legs, like someone is "brushing up" against you
- Telepathic sex with your twin
- Telepathic messages from your twin and vice versa

So now, not only do you think you're going crazy, you think you have mental *and* physical problems too. Ascension symptoms can feel much like PMS, going through menopause, or even having heart disease. But here's the thing, there's never any one symptom that lasts too long, they just kind of alternate.

During my ascension I had a period of about two weeks where my hair was super dry. I mean it was dryer than it had ever been in my whole life. I was freaking out. I have luxurious long and thick hair. I eat well and take omega-3 oils. So I was worried that my hair might break off or fall out. Then I read something about ascension symptoms and hair problems was on the list. Think about it. The crown chakra or the top of the seven chakras is your source of enlightenment and it's on the crown of your head. So it stands to reason that if your crown chakra is exploding open with all of this energy, you're bound to have some problems with your hair follicles, at least temporarily. I'm happy to say that my hair is back to normal. The extreme dryness only lasted two to three weeks, but it was scary.

Also in the early stages of metamorphosis my twin would wake me up nightly around 3 a.m. I knew it was him because I felt his energy. I sleep well normally and was getting annoyed at these nightly awakenings. Sometimes I would just shout out his name and say, "Really? What do you need to say to me? Because I really need to get some sleep now." Then I would take out a journal and write down what he needed to say. Most of the time the messages I received were very significant to what was going on or to what his soul wanted to communicate with me.

Right before our soul merging that happened on March 20, 2019, I had days at time where I was having heart palpitations that wouldn't stop. When it happens for a few minutes or an hour, you generally don't get too worried. But this was happening for days on end. During that time I was receiving a spiritual "upgrade" so I could handle the merging of our souls to where I felt his soul inside of me. I wasn't aware of it right then but on March 20th, I could backtrack and understand why the symptoms were occurring.

During this phase you will also become aligned with cosmic events. You and your twin will have a lot more coincidences during the full moon, new moon, and lunar and solar eclipses. As you're becoming more aligned with universal energy, the universe will assist you in healing and becoming more of an energetic match with each other.

One example of the universe conspiring was after I had told my twin that I loved him. We had had a deep conversation earlier in the day and it had already been five months of separation. I was fed up with the separation, but I wanted him to know how I truly felt. So I texted him that we had a soul connection, that I was in love with him, and that I loved him unconditionally. He waited a day and then texted me back something really cold. I answered that he could deny my love but he couldn't deny God's path or destiny for him, which included having me on his path. The very next day we were supposed to be in a meeting with about eight to ten people. When I arrived to the meeting, no one else was there but him. Do you believe it? God caused no one else to show up but my twin and I. Isn't that crazy? It was like God was saying to him, "She is aligned with the universe and your path together and you're not. I'm going to show you that being with her *is* your path." I was so elated that day. I thought, *You go God! You show him!*

Many wonderful and painful things are happening during this metamorphosis stage. In the next chapter I'm going to explain *why* all these changes are here to help you and your twin.

Reunion

The reunion stage is coming back together with your twin in the 3D. Many twin flame couples will go into separation, then back to union, and go right back into separation. All this means is that the learning and growing phase is not yet finished.

When you have learned all of the lessons you must learn alone and when you've ascended to a certain spiritual level, it will be time for you to reunite with your twin. If you're stuck in the mindset that says reunion is impossible, you don't understand that reunion is what God wants. You and your twin flame have been designed to come back together in this lifetime if you have met here. All you need is obedience to God and his plan. And God will handle the rest of the details. What looks impossible to you is not impossible to God. In the Bible, Luke 1:37 even says, "For with God, nothing will be impossible." Every day on YouTube I get comments from viewers explaining their impossible situations with their twin flame. For those who doubt I say now, if your twin flame is truly your twin, God already has a plan to bring you back together. In fact, you both planned this out before you came here. Do you truly believe that obstacles such as distance, culture, religion, age, marital status, job situation, or lifestyle are a shock to God? Do you think God is in the heavenly realms scratching his head going, *Wow! I'm stumped. I really don't know how to solve this one.* No. God is saying, *Stay in faith. Let me guide you. I have a plan for you and your twin flame. Trust me.*

The greatest lesson that most of us can draw from twin flame obstacles and separation is to trust in God and his infinite wisdom. If you think you have to try hard to do things to get you and your twin to come back together, you're missing the point completely. Sure, it's important that you do your spiritual homework and transcend the ego, but that is only to prepare you for reunion. All the rest is up to God and *his* divine timing.

In reality, the more you plot, manipulate, and try to control the situation to get you into reunion with your twin, generally the longer it will take. However, if you're making changes because they're right for you and your life and it happens to make things easier for you and your twin, so be it. For example, I had to leave a job because it was time for me to come into the fullness of my life purpose, but it also made things easier for my twin and me.

Reunion is not the end or culmination of the twin flame journey. It's merely the beginning. This is where the real work starts. Most twin flame couples will work together under some capacity. Many will spread spiritual messages or help other twin flame couples come into reunion. Others will start charities, blogs, YouTube channels, or conduct live seminars to spread the love. The real work will be a life of service for you and your twin. Most importantly, the service work will stem from your unconditional love for each other.

5

Stewards of Love

AT ANY STAGE IN the twin flame journey, we are ushering in love at all levels. The best place to start is with self-love. As someone with a healthy dose of self-confidence, I thought I had a lot of self-love. Even though I loved myself, my behavior and choices didn't always reflect that. I had decades of unhealthy love relationships before I realized that if I loved myself fully, I wouldn't have subjected myself to that. In the midst of all these relationships, I mistakenly thought I could fix them or fix the relationship instead of seeking out a person who was worthy of me. And those thoughts came from a deeply rooted insecurity that says, *I am not worthy of receiving a healthy person who is whole. All I'm worth is a completely broken person who isn't able to pull their weight in a relationship, so I have to hold the weight for two.* Do you see how completely messed up that mentality is? Even in the midst of my twin flame journey in separation, I had the following thoughts; *Maybe I'm not good enough for him. Maybe I just need to go back to my previous relationship because I can't do any better.* In all fairness to the man I was with before my twin, he is awesome in many ways and we are still friends to this day. It's just that our learning and growing was lopsided most of the time with me doing most of the teaching and growing and with him absorbing. In a healthy relationship you need a balance of both giving and receiving that will flip back and forth. Healthiness never keeps the burden on one or the same side of the couple most of the time. So in order to balance the scales and be able to have the game of pitch and catch where you both play pitcher and catcher, self-love is a good place to start. But first, let's define what it means to love unconditionally.

Defining Unconditional Love

A good place to turn to for a definition of unconditional love is a Bible passage often quoted at weddings, 1 Corinthians 13.

> *Love is patient and kind. Love is not jealous or boastful or proud. It does not demand its own way. It is not irritable, and it keeps no record of being wronged. It does not rejoice about injustice but rejoices whenever the truth wins out. Love never gives up, never loses faith, is always hopeful and endures through every circumstance. (1 Corinthians 13:4-7 NLT)*

If you read on, *1 Corinthians 14:1 says, Let love be your highest goal.*

The captivating part of this is that even though it's read at most weddings, rare is the couple who absorbs the words and puts them into action. In fact, think about all of your relationships, not just the romantic ones. When was the last time you practiced all of the traits of unconditional love? It's not an easy thing to do.

Let's just take one trait, *It does not demand its own way.* I can remember in the beginning of our connection, I was not only impatient with my twin but I also demanded my own way, a lot. All of that came out of fear. In your twin flame connection, how many times have you wanted things to go your own way? For example, have you wanted your twin to change on your timeline?

Even though humans are imperfect and most have not showed us the path to unconditional love, God has shown us. We might even say we don't have a handbook for loving unconditionally. But look in earnest at the passage above. God has made it pretty clear by using words of emphasis such as "is", "not", "always", and "never."

Imagine what it would be like to never give up on your twin, to never lose faith, and to endure through every circumstance with your twin. Just imagine the type of love that develops through that kind of commitment. It would be nothing less than phenomenal.

Now let's imagine giving yourself that kind of love.

The Elevation of Self-Love

You are worthy of every good thing on this earth. Many of us come from a place where we've been taught to not want too much. We have heard phrases like, "You're selfish." "What do you think? That we're made of money?" Or "Have a back-up plan just in case your dreams fall through." In like manner, the following is the best soul-crushing comment, "Stop asking!" *Stop Asking! What? Why?* The Bible itself says, "Ask and you shall receive." "Knock and the door will be opened." "Seek and you will find." Another phrase most of us have heard growing up is, "You don't deserve it." I hear parents say it to their kids all the time. "You don't deserve that cookie. You haven't earned it." Holy cow! What are we doing to people's sense of self-love. Jesus said of the God the Father, "It is my Father's pleasure to give you the kingdom." Jesus didn't say, "Nope, you don't deserve it. You haven't been good today."

God wants to give you his kingdom and that includes everything good. Loving yourself means holding esteem that you're worthy to receive all that is good. The only thing you need is to be you. That's it. Nothing more. And when you get that and really get it on the inside, you'll start to have more self-respect and compassion for everything that you are. God didn't say, "I won't give you the kingdom unless your chakras are aligned or until you give all of your money to the poor and meditate for six hours a day." He said happily, "My kingdom is yours."

Receiving All That You Are

You are beautiful, awesome, amazing, and talented. You are a loving child of the most High God. You are also human with flaws and shortcomings. (Wow! That statement didn't feel as good as the first two did it?) But in order to have a full healthy dose of self-love, you must accept all of you including all of your flaws and shortcomings. For many of us, that's where we fall short. We tentatively accept our gifts, talents, and positive traits and shamefully brush under the rug the things we don't like about ourselves. When we do this, we only love ourselves partially. Then when those things we don't like come creeping out from under the rug (because they always do), we feel ashamed and unworthy. But when you embrace all of who you are, nothing can come lurking out of the shadows because everything is already in the light. For example, if you react angrily to a co-worker, give that part of you a hug and say, *It's okay I love the part of you that reacts with anger.* (And give yourself a loving pat on the back.) It makes that part of you go, *Huh? Um, what's happening?* The reason this works is because the part of you, who reacts with anger, is used to hearing, *Why do you react that way? You're supposed to be a loving person. You're not doing a good enough job of that. You're a bad person.* Do you feel the difference?

Being Afraid of Unconditional Love

Fear comes in all shapes and sizes. We all crave love. We all spend our lives searching for love. We are consumers of romance novels, romantic comedies, love songs, poems, reality shows on love, and real-life romance videos. The concept of love obsesses us. But in reality, most of us are afraid of love.

As I mentioned, the first conversation my twin flame and I had was about marriage. He confirmed, in that conversation, he was thinking that same morning about marriage and having a wife. In later conversations he talked about his knowledge of romantic relationships and to his friends he was considered a "relationship expert." We even talked about a relationship book we liked in common. Yet when push came to shove he told me, "I don't want a relationship." It's that type of incongruence that plagues many of us.

We dream about love. We crave it. Nonetheless, when true love comes to us we often shut the door. Why is that?

I believe it's because most of us for most of our lives have experienced a very conditional type of love. True unconditional love is rare to come by, so when it does, we don't recognize it or it scares us. We have a tendency to think that if someone loves us unconditionally that there must be something wrong with *them*. Or we sit around waiting for the other shoe to drop. For this reason we begin looking for flaws in the other person or we exaggerate their shortcomings. True love is so pure and rare that some can see it as an abnormality. Books and movies further this belief with romantic comedies showing love riddled with problems until the very end. And in the movies where you see a person truly in love, it usually depicts a psychopath obsessed with another person until they murder them in the end. Does you see how messed up that is?

Not only are most of us not well equipped to receive unconditional love, but also a fair amount of us aren't well versed in how to give unconditional love. It's as if someone gifts us a brand-new $200,000 manual-shift car, with all the bells and whistles, and we have no idea how to work it. We want to make this sleek new car run fast and smooth, yet we don't even have the know-how to get it out of first gear. Therefore, we end up flubbing it up, *a lot*, along the way.

Going Back to Our Comfort Zone

The love I grew up with was very conditional. It was dysfunctional and twisted. The love I received was also inconsistent and chaotic. It had high highs and rock bottom lows. As a result, I was lonely much of the time as a child. I felt my parents were too wrapped up in their own problems to be emotionally available for me. Therefore, it's no surprise that the relationships I chose had this same type of love. For example, having someone love me like crazy then push me away felt very normal to me. Or having a person point out my flaws and tell me that I'm not good enough (on some level) felt comfortable. In addition, being immersed in drama felt passionate and dramatic. But that isn't the case any more.

The reason why some of us continually return to dysfunctional relationships is because we aren't able to receive healthy ones. On some level they don't compute. Just as you might have a difficult time receiving unconditional love, your twin flame might too. And the measure to which you are fighting an unconditionally loving relationship is the level at which you are still infused in your childhood wounds.

Releasing That Which Is Familiar to You

In order to give and receive unconditional love you must jump out of your comfort zone. Our impressions from childhood are deeply rooted in who we are. Most of the time we're not aware that we're choosing partners who are repeating patterns from the past. Then when the similarities creep up, we're left thinking, *Oh no! Not again!*

A great exercise to help you get clear on what you will and won't tolerate is to make a list of relationship behaviors that don't work for you. Once you have this list, be aware of the signs of those forbidden traits. For example, I don't tolerate someone who lies. I grew up with parents who constantly lied and deceived and I don't tolerate lying at all. Yet I found myself with romantic partners who lied a lot. In a long-term relationship after my divorce, the person started out the relationship lying about his age. About six weeks into the relationship I found out his real age, that was five years older than me. At the time I got angry, but I didn't heed the red flag and continued to date him. Throughout our time together I discovered that he lied about many things. In the end, it was my fault for staying with someone who lied because I refused to see that flaw.

When it comes to your twin flame relationship you may not be able to pick and choose the person's personality flaws. After all, we've already established that your souls were split before birth. But what you can control is when you choose to reunite with your twin. You can hold off until they work on their changeable flaws such as an addiction, dishonesty, cheating, or lack of follow-through to give a few examples.

You might now be thinking, *But isn't that setting conditions to love?* The answer is, "No". I didn't say to not love your twin. I said to allow them to learn and grow by themselves and get rid of their shortcomings before coming into reunion with them. You can still love them from afar. You just don't have to put up with their crap.

Remember the mirroring effect of the twin flame connection I discussed? God knows your childhood and relationship wounds. When your twin "shows up" with traits you can't tolerate, it's mirroring back to you what you haven't worked out. For example, because of my past two relationships I will not tolerate a man who drinks alcohol or does drugs of any kind. The moment I met my twin he told me he didn't drink. To me, that was confirmation that I had worked out that part of my life and that I no longer needed to be with someone who drank.

Often what we do, in a guise to be loving, is to accept the unacceptable to get the relationship we want. Then, when the person starts to act in a way we can't accept, we blame them instead of holding ourselves responsible for not holding a space of self-love.

Giving and Receiving Unconditional Love

First of all, I'm going to assume you've heard the expression; *You can't give away what you don't have.* This statement is especially true when it comes to unconditional love. Both the divine feminine and divine masculine alike must work through issues of self-love before they're able to give love unconditionally to their twin. However, the divine feminine collective tends to have to work on it a little more. By nature the divine feminine is nurturing, giving, and loving. It's not hard for her to do this. It almost comes as naturally as breathing. The more challenging part is giving love to herself.

Historically the feminine collective has been trained to give without receiving and also give until she has nothing left. Furthermore, the feminine has been brought up to be the weaker party and therefore, the victim or martyr. Centuries of this social acceptance have created a huge energetic imbalance in the universe. We as the divine feminine collective in the 21st century are here to break that pattern. We're here to show the world that we can be rooted in feminine energy *and* be powerful.

As twin flame couples, we are here to advance unconditional love in the world. The first step begins with loving ourselves unconditionally, then moving into loving your twin flame unconditionally, and finally to loving the world unconditionally.

Self-love

Throughout this work, we're going to intensely focus on what it means to evolve into unshakable self-love. For this is the root of all forms of unconditional love.

Loving Your Twin

Not having had many role models to display unconditional love, most of us don't know how to give it completely. What we believe is unconditional love is usually a form of love with conditions. Often this comes about as we try to mold a person to fit our idea of what a relationship should be like instead of letting that person be his or herself. Unconditionally loving your twin means unconditionally accepting who he or she is with every asset and flaw. Unconditionally loving your twin also means you love them for who they are and not who you want them to be. Many of us are used to getting into fixer-upper relationships where we think it's our job to fix them. God handpicked your true twin flame for you. They are perfect the way they are, even with all of their flaws. Your job is not to fix them. Your job is to love them. In this love you understand who your twin is and that they are on a unique path to learning certain lessons that may or may not include you.

Unconditional love is infinite patience, joy, compassion, empathy, understanding, and freedom. In unconditional love, you give your twin the freedom to be him or herself in every moment. You never try to control them or their lives. And you never try to control the relationship.

Understandably this goes in direct opposition to most everything we're taught in relationships. We're taught to love and never let go. In couples therapy we're taught to talk about *our* needs, wants, and desires. In the same fashion, most TV shows demonstrate couples manipulating each other to get their own way. Additionally, many advice-giving talk shows highlight relationship experts explaining how to point out your partner's flaws, how they wronged you, or how they must change their behavior. I'm certain that the intent is not inherently bad. However, advice as such keeps us in a cycle of blame and ego-centeredness. A relationship then becomes about getting "my needs met" only and doesn't take into consideration a person's freewill to act as they choose.

Obviously a fine line exists between letting a romantic partner walk all over you and attempting to control them. When you come from a place of unconditional self-love coupled with unconditional love for your romantic partner, you're able to differentiate between these two polarities. For example, if your romantic partner is talking to you in a way you deem as harsh, you can simply say, "I'm not feeling great in this conversation right now. I'm going to remove myself from this and we can pick it up when I'm feeling better. Okay?" In that example, you're giving yourself the self-love you need and giving your partner the love they need. You're not judging or blaming them. You're simply taking responsibility for your feelings and for what's going on inside of you.

A question that may arise out of this explanation is, "What if my twin flame continues to have behavior I can't accept?" Honestly, you can create physical distance between you and your twin until they decide to change their behavior. Creating distance does not mean you are less loving. On the contrary, it means you are more loving. As an unconditionally loving person you are recognizing how to treat others and also how you want to be treated. By preemptively holding a space of love for a negative situation, you're dispelling any darkness that may get in your way.

Most people stay in a negative situation while creating a lot of animosity for both parties. You're hurting, so you try to manipulate or control the other person. Then they are hurting and they lash out or ignore you.

A twin flame romantic relationship will cause situations and circumstances where you are forced to act in a way that sets boundaries in the beginning. Since the relationship is designed to purge out all of your emotional wounds, you will see some undesirable behavior. Depending on you and your twin's spiritual evolution, the negative behavior may be more or less.

Loving your twin unconditionally also means you hold nothing back from them. I remember going through my dark night of the soul, when my twin and I were in separation, and I was faced with my own fears and demons. At that time I thought about union with my twin and us sharing our lives together. Those thoughts brought me to thinking about division of duties, bills, money etc. Then I got an epiphany. For me the epiphany was, *I must give everything to my twin and not hold back anything. Everything I am and everything I have must be ours.* Now this was a big deal for me. I had been in abusive relationships in the past. To protect myself I had to partition my life and my assets. In the midst of those relationships it was a necessary defense mechanism. But in this awakened moment God was telling me, *Your twin is different. You can trust him completely. He will hold nothing back from you and you are to hold nothing back from him.* At those words I immediately wrote a journal entry to my twin telling him

I would hold nothing back from him. Upon writing it, I felt an immense sense of freedom. For, in my life, I had never felt I could trust anyone with every part of me, yet I now felt it with him.

Loving the World Unconditionally

When you're able to move through the stages of unconditional love from unconditional self-love to unconditionally loving your twin, you extend that love outward to the world. My twin is much better than me at this one. He is patient, forgiving, and kind. I am naturally a little more impatient and can have a tendency to hold on to certain things.

Loving the world unconditionally means you let the world be as it is. It also means you do what you can to spread love to the world each day. Spreading love can mean giving smiles, compliments, or prayers. It can also mean buying a coffee and muffin for the homeless person in front of your local coffee shop. Additionally you can spread your love by cleaning up your local beach, volunteering at the animal shelter, or buying an electric car.

Moreover, loving unconditionally means practicing non-judgment and acceptance. In our ego-centeredness we can sometimes assert that the world must fit into what we believe it should be.

One day my 15-year-old son and I were coming back from a beach walk. On the sidewalk in front of me I saw a dog that had just pooped. "Ugh!" I said out loud and moved to the bike lane in the street. My son said, "Why did you move?" I answered, "Because the dog pooped on the sidewalk!" Then as we advanced some more, a guy exhaled his cigarette smoke right next to us. Annoyed, I waved away the cloud of smoke. Again my son said, "Mom, what are you doing?" I answered, "Ugh! That guy was smoking!" Like the little Buddha he is, my son replied calmly as he patted me on the back, "Welcome to being human mom. This is planet earth. Dogs poop. And people smoke. Welcome." Indeed, he had a point. Sometimes I forget what it is to be human and to accept that the world as it is. The annoying things of the world are not here to annoy me per se; they're just present as a part of the world. And it's in accepting everything, as it is that I can learn to love the world more unconditionally.

In the following chapters we'll learn how to transcend the ego to be able to love more fully.

6

Divine Masculine, Divine Feminine, Divine Sex?

*T*HE DYNAMIC OF THE twin flame duo is often a confusing and debated one. The depth of the energetic dynamic goes way beyond what words can describe. And the necessary healing process is integrated into the polarity of the connection. Therefore, it's important that you grasp the differences between the divine feminine, divine masculine, and understand why a sexual relationship is essential in a twin flame romantic relationship.

As I've mentioned in all of the other chapters in this book, rather than staying focused on gender and physical body, when I outline differences in the divine masculine or feminine, I'm focusing on energy. To that end, I will use adjectives and nouns to help you understand the essence of each of the energies. Therefore, it doesn't matter if you have a man or woman's body. It matters not if you are heterosexual, homosexual, bisexual, transgender, or don't identify with a gender. What matters is the polarity between you and your twin. Many, who may have been previously confused about where they fit in when it comes to the physical world, often find that they find more clarity when energies are balanced between them and their twin.

Furthermore, it's equally important for you to know the difference and purpose so that you can come into harmonious reunion with your twin flame. Because of the demands of society and also the latest trends, fads, and social movements, many twins find themselves absorbing and embodying both energies strongly. For the sake of your connection with your twin flame, you will always have an inherent dominant energy and your twin will have the opposite energy. Once you are both healed and in complete union, those energies might swap from time to time. Or you can both healthfully integrate both feminine and masculine energies and transcend them altogether. But that is only when you've reached a place of spiritual mastery that comes naturally after you've done all the work and healing that will bring and keep you together.

Pay close attention to this lesson and notice any feelings of resistance that arise within you as you read it. In

Divine Masculine, Divine Feminine, Divine Sex?

2019, we are living in a time where modern society has rejected the notion of gender and therefore traditional male/female roles. The end goal of this movement was to help break through prejudice and traditional models of gender roles. But instead what has happened is an utter confusion of what reality holds in the entire animal kingdom leaving us more baffled than ever. Modern new parents are now letting their kids decide their gender instead of raising them to be a little boy or girl. The lines between sexual preferences have become fluid and experimental in young children who are still forming their concept of the world around them and their own inclinations. While the intentions were in a good place, the outcomes are creating a generation with no well-defined boundaries, which adds to the general confusion about life in general. The truth is, in the physical world boundaries do exist. Polarity and differences exist not only between male and female but also between masculine and feminine energies. To say that differences don't exist is to question the source that created you and the rest of the world. The reason why so many twin flame couples are having a hard time and thus, are staying in separation is because they refuse to see this principle of polarity. Therefore, the resistance you might be feeling may be coming from modern-day social conditioning and nothing else.

The words I use to describe the respective energies will sound like a traditional masculine or feminine role in life. Your energy and the one that resonates with you will help you determine where you are on your twin flame journey. And it will help you understand your twin flame in his or her journey too. To further the explanation I will integrate a small description of the chakra system and show you that even within your own body, the dynamic dance of masculine and feminine energies exist.

Divine Feminine

The divine feminine is the creative force out of which everything emanates. The impulse to create is the desire that lies within divine feminine energy. The keyword here is *desire*. The feminine is the yearning for expansion. It wants to see beautiful things grow out of nothingness. According to ancient East Indian texts, a formless energy first existed called *purusha* and out of purusha came *prakruti* or nature or form. In other words, God existed and he had the desire to create and therefore created. The formless expansive energy is the divine feminine and the force to create is the divine masculine.

Words to describe feminine energy are as follows:

Beauty	Compassion	Empathy	Nurturing
Magnetic	Voluptuous	Adorning	Joyful
Laughter	Shy/ Bashful	Lunar	Passive
Receiving	Soft skin	Sattvic	Receptive

Divine Masculine, Divine Feminine, Divine Sex?

Unconditional Love	Holding Space	Quiet Strength	Melodious Voice
Flowing	Playful	Gentle	Connecting
Yin	Soft	Humble	Alluring
Graceful	Forgiving	Patient	Cooling

These words are present to help give you a mental picture of the energy the divine feminine embodies. They aren't here to limit your vision but to enhance it.

As we tie in the understanding of the feminine energy to the chakra system, we can further grasp the whole of it. The seven main chakras that align the spine have alternating energies until you get to the sixth chakra, which integrates the energies. The second and fourth chakras hold the most feminine energy while the first, third, and fifth hold more of the masculine energy.

The second chakra located in the area above the pubic bone and below the navel, is the sexual and creativity chakra. Herein lies the "womb of creation". Through the second or sacral chakra the impulse is not only to create a baby, but also to create anything out of nothing. The fourth chakra is the heart center and the source of love, compassion, empathy, and forgiveness. It is also the center of playfulness, joy, and laughter.

As you may begin to see, this energy is gentle but powerful. It's an energy that takes its time. Through quiet patience something beautiful arises.

I'm not a person who enjoys the winter. For most of my life I lived in colder climates where winter almost never seemed to end. I would impatiently await the spring, the beauty of the first spring flowers, and the warmth of increasing daylight. I remember one February, in particular, that had been brutally harsh, dark, and cold. Depression had overcome me and I sat outside just waiting for something to move me out of my mood. At once I looked down and noticed little green shoots coming out of a flowerbed. Those little plants, later to become daffodils, gave me hope and to me, they couldn't grow fast enough.

Women awaiting the birth of a child also know that creative energy takes time, patience, and quiet strength. After about 32 weeks gestation, most women are done. They just want the pregnancy to be over and to see their baby. But if the baby comes at 32 weeks, the newborn sometimes has health problems such as less than fully developed lungs. So the pregnant mom must wait until the baby is full term, often in discomfort and pain.

Feminine energy is beautiful and magical. Yet modern life often views it as weak and inefficient. Let's go back to the example of having a baby. The creative force of life has a natural timeline. In recent decades, modern science has not liked nature's timeline. So modern medicine has forced calculated birth on expectant moms for the sake of "safety" and "security", in other words, for convenience. More women than ever are induced into childbirth or have scheduled Cesarean sections. Let's entertain another example. Walking into a tropical rainforest you'll see abundantly growing and colorful plant and animal life. God works wonders to balance the ecosystem in his own time and creative plan. No one walks into a natural rainforest and says, "Damn, this is so messy. We need to clean up the joint." Most who experience the beauty are blown away. Yet our modern farming practices claim that we can do nature better. So we have created chemicals to grow plants and animals better, faster, bigger, and with more yield. As a result of this *yang* energy where *yin* energy must be present, we have polluted and destroyed our planet.

In the same token, naturally occurring *yin* or feminine energy exists in about half of the human population. To get to twin flame reunion, find which energy you embody and embrace it like you own it.

For the divine feminine it can sometimes be difficult to tell if you're truly divine feminine. We live in a very yang or masculine world. So sometimes you could be divine feminine but your environment has caused you to adapt to and adopt more masculine energy. To get to your core energy try meditating daily twice per day and you'll start to see your true energy emerge.

Divine Masculine

A forward-moving energy, yang or masculine energy goes toward. Goal-oriented accomplishments are a result of masculine energy. As I mentioned, most of the modern world today operates through masculine energy. The great earthly imbalance is caused by the forcefulness of yang energy pushing through and into places where yin energy needs to be. Let's take for example childhood. Most of childhood is a yin or feminine energy time. Even though a child is growing quickly, it's a time of creativity and playful exploration. A child's imagination is at its height and energy is flowing freely. The boundless, limitless child feels their way through life with an open heart. Love is abundant. Forgiveness is quick. Affection is given freely. Yet, modern adults, with the best intentions of making "smart" kids who are going to get good jobs and make decent money, push these perfect creations into adult-like roles way too quickly. So as "good" modern parents, we push our kids into supervised and scheduled activities, teach them four new languages, and put them into computer programming classes by age five. Then we wonder why so many kids have ADD, ADHD, and are on the autism spectrum. Well, in part it's because we push our kids away from their natural energy into an energy they're not ready to live in. They have internal hardwiring that says, "You are to be free to explore, create, examine, move, and be energetic and boundless." But we say to them, "Live in masculine energy. Be focused, competitive, task oriented, and disciplined." By doing that to these naturally beautifully created and intuitive beings, we're messing with their hardwiring and then we wonder why they can't cope with life.

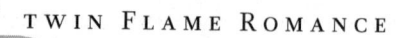

Divine Masculine, Divine Feminine, Divine Sex?

If a child is allowed to freely explore who they are in childhood without too much interference, their natural energetic propensity will emerge. Some who have an inherently strong amount of masculine energy will show up as kids who have a competitive drive and will naturally excel in certain active tasks. They might be more aggressive or assertive and with proper guidance they can channel that energy nicely to enhance it.

Masculine energy is needed as much as feminine energy. It's an earthly balance that must be respected. Even though we all possess both energies, those who have more masculine energy may see these inherent qualities.

Driven	Forward-moving	Penetrating	Hot
Warm	Energetic	Solar	Aggressive
Assertive	Physically strong	Problem-solving	Calculating
Unemotional	Logical	Focused	Single task-oriented
Driving force	Goal-oriented	Moving	Giving
Providing	Intense	Competitive	Enterprising
Passionate	Hunting	Searching	Rajasic

The first, third, and fifth chakras come into play with masculine energy. The first chakra is the root and takes care of security on earth and getting your basic needs met. Next, the third chakra is about pushing outward into the world to assert your will and get goals accomplished through a sense of personal power. Finally the fifth chakra is about vocalizing your highest truth and speaking to the world.

When you have balanced one, you've balanced them all. Let me give you an example in sports. If you're a tennis player and your backhand is naturally strong, a good coach won't encourage you to ignore your strength and focus on your lesser quality first. A talented coach will make you develop your backhand so it's even stronger until your strength becomes unstoppable. After you've mastered your natural talent, the coach will then help you work on your weaknesses. He'll do this because he knows it will take time, energy, and consistency. The same goes for practicing your energetic muscle. If your natural propensity is to have more masculine energy, develop that until it's the highest and best version of the divine masculine. Then work on integrating divine feminine energy where it's appropriate. In a twin flame connection your twin will help you do this naturally. My twin taught me this by barely saying a word.

Throughout our separation, I was embodying more masculine energy between us and I'm naturally much more feminine. But I would do things that were rooted in yang energy. For example, I would text him out of frustration or in exasperation I would say something like, "We have to meet for coffee to continue this conversation." He would gently withdraw from me when this happened which was his way of saying, "Michelle, energetically you're not where you're supposed to be."

Divine Masculine, Divine Feminine, Divine Sex?

When I would go back to holding the feminine energetic space, he would always come to me. Since he is my divine masculine, I couldn't possibility hold in domination both the masculine *and* feminine energies, because that would hold no space for him.

The Balance of Polarity

Finding your inherent nature is but one aspect of twin flame attraction. As you ease back into your natural state energetically, healing is taking place all along the way. You're healing your childhood wounds, past relationships, and past lives. In addition you're raising the vibrational consciousness for the entire divine feminine or divine masculine collectivity. In later chapters we'll discuss more about healing. For now we'll start with sexual union with your twin as a means to heal.

Twin Flame Sex

Sex is a necessary and important part of a twin flame relationship. For most twin flame couples, this aspect comes easily. Twin flames typically find that the attraction is so undeniably strong that they can't keep their hands off of each other. I mentioned, in part of my story, that I wasn't initially attracted to my twin. Yet once we started talking about dating and he mentioned physical attraction, my attraction to him awakened. On the inside I somehow knew I was attracted to him all along. Then the next time I saw him I could only think about how incredibly attractive he was to me. When we got together it was explosive fireworks. Even though I had had some great intimate relationships in the past, nothing compared to how I felt when I was with him. It was totally different in almost every way. The only way to describe it is that our energy completely matched and synergized together. I never knew I could feel excited and at peace at the same time and that's what happened with my twin.

You may have a similar story with your twin flame. And it's a good thing too. You are doing more than giving and receiving pleasure. You are exchanging energy and information to heal and awaken to higher states of consciousness.

Many have claimed that twin flames don't need to be in a sexual relationship, I would argue that nothing could be further from the truth. Since the twin flame relationship is designed to experience every aspect and flavor of life, it stands to reason that sex must be a part of this romantic connection.

Shattering Paradigms

As you might recall in some of my earlier explanations, much of the twin flame journey is about shattering outdated paradigms that don't serve us anymore. For centuries, if not the entirety of recorded human history, sex has been given a bad name. Even though God created us as sexual creatures, a stigma has always been attached to it. Sex is seen as dirty, forbidden, shameful, nasty, and as something that must be hidden. As a result, it has

Divine Masculine, Divine Feminine, Divine Sex?

grown into a negative massive obsession in mainstream society. The more you suppress something, the bigger it becomes. And sex has been suppressed for a long time. Instead of being attached to a natural and normal human need, it's seen as abnormal or even scornful. Even in marriage, from the outside it's talked about in hushed tones. Some religions try to emphasize that the only need for sex is to procreate.

Then we get into even more confusing sexual paradigms of infidelity or people believing they can't be faithful to one person. The intense intimacy between two people is strong, open, vulnerable, and binding. The profound work we must do within ourselves comes only as a result of the strong commitment and bond we have with one other person and in this case, our twin.

For those who claim that they can't be monogamous or have too much love to give to just one person, they are simply confused about the sanctity of a sexual relationship. It takes a spiritual badass to commit to one person sexually and reap the benefits of that connection. The ego wants you to believe otherwise.

Your twin flame is a perfect fit for you inside and out. The work you need to do with your twin happens as much sexually as it does on other levels. The transcendence past your ego into unconditional love is only possible when you are willing to give 100% to your twin and not hold back a single cell of who you are. Even people who are "faithful" to their spouse still hold back.

They use sex as a weapon, punishment, or reward. The training ground for unconditional love in a twin flame relationship is that you both learn to willingly give everything to each other. And when you come to the space where you give everything to your twin, with no reticence whatsoever, your twin will intuitively know what is good for the both of you. Based on your past I know you might be thinking, *Hold nothing back? Well, what if I'm tired or stressed? Am I supposed to give in to sex with my twin even then?* The answer to that concern is unfounded because twin flames are in a different space when it comes to intimacy, therefore, those concerns won't even be present. For example, you and your twin will be so in sync that when you're tired, your twin will intuitively say, "Lie down. Let me give you a back rub." And then you will drift off to sleep in the bliss of a wonderful back rub.

In other words, sex, intimacy, and commitment to your twin will come naturally. You won't need to obsess or think about it. The energy will just flow between the two of you. And all of that comes from the place of selfless love.

The balancing of the divine feminine and divine masculine energies as well as the transcendence of the ego work together to help you and your twin find the right steps to enter into the dynamic dance together. Instead of crushing each other's toes or bumping awkwardly,

Divine Masculine, Divine Feminine, Divine Sex?

you'll soon find that you're gliding gracefully across the dance floor of life together in synchronistic harmony.

ns and different
The Work: How You Transform

*I*N ORDER TO COME into full reunion, twin flames must be an energetic match. That is, they must fit together on all levels. Because you and your twin have lived different lives and different past lives, you've collected diverse impressions, experiences, karma, and memories. When you hear twin flame communities speak of *the work*, they're referring to the purging of past energetic stuff you no longer need in order to have a squeaky clean slate to come together.

Think of transitional life moments such as having a baby or selling a home. As we prepare for these major life shifts, we often do a thorough cleaning or purging. We may throw away items, give them away, or sell them. We usually clean everything to create space for the new baby or for potential buyers to walk through our home, for example. During "the work" phase, you're internally preparing for reunion with your twin. You may even be doing some external preparation as well.

For you to better understand what happens from an internal standpoint, let's look at the layers of you and who you are.

The Layers of You

For this lesson, I'm going to briefly introduce a concept related to yoga philosophy. This is something I teach in my meditation classes in depth. But here we're going to touch on it superficially so you can bridge to what you do know.

We are comprised of several layers. We have a physical body, this incarnation of flesh and bones, which is directly dependent on and influenced by its environment. Next we have our energy body, which surrounds the physical body at all times. People who read auras see the energy body. Those with a fully awakened energy body appear to have a halo surrounding them, especially around the crown chakra. The third physical layer is the environment. The environment can be Mother Earth, your home, car, family, society, job, and other people.

Then you have your mind, intellect, and ego. Your mind is what we refer to as our thoughts. Many of us have a monkey mind. We think thousands of thoughts a day. They flit to and fro and seem to be relatively chaotic. Our minds can sometimes drive us crazy and are often the source of many mental illnesses. Next we have the intellect. That is the layer of discernment. The intellect is always judging. It's dividing things to help you make choices. Otherwise you'd always be in a constant state of indecision. The next layer, the ego, is the one that causes us many problems. It's a necessary part of who we are, but it's also the most constricted part. In this chapter we'll explore the roles of the mind, intellect, and ego in transcendence.

Finally you have your individual soul (which you share with your twin flame), the collective soul, and the universal soul. Your individual soul is a collection of your experiences, karma, and your soul purpose. The collective soul gathers aspects of the collectivity of all souls currently incarnated on earth. While we are a part of the greater collectivity of souls, we are also part of a subset of souls. The twin flame community of the 21st century, or more particularly of 2019 and beyond, is a strong collectivity of souls designed to propel the entire collective forward toward unconditional love.

Ultimately we have the universal soul, which is God consciousness. It's all things. It's the essence of all that is. Universal soul is all pervasive, all knowing, and ever present. It has no beginnings and no endings. It is never bound by space, time, and causality. You are universal soul and so am I. But first, we are here, now. And we must learn to live with all of the other layers.

The Conditionality of Human Existence

When you are an earth angel or lightworker, which we all are in this twin flame journey, it can be very difficult to understand the conditionality of life. You come here with so much love, openness, and willingness to help and be of service, that when life hits you with conditions, it's confusing.

You arrive as a being of light with open arms and say, "I'm here!" And someone shuts the door in your face. Then you begin to doubt who you are and why you're here in the first place. The more you encounter conditional situations and people, the more you fall into self-doubt. Inside you *know* who you are and what you're meant to do on earth. But because the world cannot and will not accept you as you are, you begin to build up walls. These walls are called your ego.

As lightworkers we learn to take on an ego. Most of us in this collective are not born with much of an ego. But boy oh boy, each time a door is shut in our face we learn that in order to survive on earth, we must build up our ego muscles. And it feels uncomfortable because we know it's wrong for us. So a majority of lightworkers live in constant conflict with themselves their whole lives.

Another part of the collectivity, which will call "normal people" just for the sake of conversation, are born with a healthy amount of ego. Normal people come into this world with a fair amount of karma and a small amount of spiritual awareness. These people understand the world and know exactly how to act to fit in. They rarely have issues or problems with following rules or forging their earthly path. They do what must be done. They go to school, get jobs, buy homes, go on vacation, raise families, are sports fans, and have a 401K. If you ask them why they're here, they say, "YOLO!" or "Live your best life." Or even, "Life's a bitch and then you die. Hey, do you want a beer?"

When I was with my alcoholic boyfriend, I was miserable for years as I tried to "save his soul". Meanwhile, he was having a great time. Seriously, he was the one with the problem, I was trying to help him, and *I* was the one miserable, not him. His ego was telling him, "Hey, have fun. Live it up. YOLO!" and I was like, "Aren't you worried about your life purpose and living for God?" That was the byproduct of different souls, purposes, and aspects of existence. Also, those who come here with ego tend to be more accepting of the journey of life than those of us who are lightworkers.

Accepting the conditionality of life *is* part of our journey as lightworkers. We agreed to take on this human life whether we remember it or not. And the more we fight it, the more difficult it becomes. The truth is *most* lightworkers fight it. They say things like, "I don't want to be selfish. I don't need to make that much money as long as I'm happy. I don't need that much to survive. It doesn't matter to me, whatever you want. I want to be the loving and selfless one." Meanwhile we get bulldozed over by normal people who are trying to get ahead.

Who said you couldn't live your life existence *and* be wealthy and happy? Who said you don't deserve to be in great relationships *and* have a great job? No one but you ever said that. God certainly didn't say that when he sent you down here. Do you understand that you're the only one telling you all of that malarkey?

As a result, many lightworkers end up worse than normal people. They have bigger egos, more problems, less money, awful relationships, and more confusion. The reason is because they deny who they are and fail to accept human conditionality.

Defining Human Conditionality

You came here to earth and agreed to live life here. In order to live successfully and fully you need to accept certain things. As lightworkers, most of us have one foot in heaven and the other on earth and are not quite sure how to navigate living both. Since earth life is often painful, we opt to live a half-assed life and spend more time in heavenly existence. But that's not what we're meant to do! We're meant to live enlightened spiritual lives while immersing ourselves fully in this earthly life. We are designed to literally bring heaven to Earth.

In this human existence we have duality. That means we have a life of opposites. We have to learn to take the

The Work: How You Transform

good and the bad, cranky people and good people, or fun jobs and really boring ones sometimes. So many flavors of life exist. Life presents hundreds of thousands of experiences for you to enjoy. Why wouldn't you want to experience them all?

I've done quite a lot in my life and have had some intensely different and zany experiences. I've studied acting, psychology, journalism, law, education, Spanish, French, German, Ayurvedic medicine, Vedanta, real estate, and those are just majors. In addition I've traveled the world and lived in other countries. I've taken many, many risks, some of which I realize now may have been too risky, but I tend to embrace life as it comes. Many ask me how it's possible that I've had so many varied life experiences and the real answer is that there is not much I refuse to experience. That being said, I have suffered from the lightworker syndrome of not being present where I'm at all the time. And that was mostly due to my karmic lessons.

Conditionality of human existence means you agreed to come here and go to school and do work so you can get paid to do things like buy food, have shelter, support a family perhaps, and live in a society. Coming from the perfection of heaven, many lightworkers have a hard time understanding this. That's why many of them are not "successful" as they are measured to society's standards. They feel like they don't quite fit in and tend to be the outliers of society. As a result many suffer from anxiety, depression, and other mental illnesses because there is incongruence with how they feel and what's expected of them.

In order to embrace the conditionality of human existence, you must give yourself permission to live here now. It's okay to taste the flavors of life. Enjoy a work softball team, even if you're bad at playing. Go to the family picnics even if everyone thinks you're weird. Be who you are fully and love the wholeness of who you are.

Embrace the Law of Karma

The law of karma is a simple concept. You've likely heard the expression, "What goes around comes around." Right? The law of karma means every action generates a reaction. The reaction can be positive, negative, or neutral. Positive actions create good karma while negative actions create a debt that must be repaid. Neutral actions generally don't generate one or the other. For example, making the bed could be a positive action if you live with someone who enjoys a made bed but if you live alone, it might be a neutral action since it's not necessarily impacting anyone.

Throughout our lives we've accumulated some karmic debt that must be repaid. And if you believe in past lives, we've also brought forth karmic debts to repay in this lifetime. At times we also serve as a catalyst so that others can repay their karmic debts. If you have had a

The Work: How You Transform

string of negative things happen to you, you might be thinking, *Why does bad luck always come to me? I'm a good person.* The likely answer is the repayment of karmic debt.

Another reason we can feel like we're constantly on an uphill battle in life is because we haven't developed the awareness to get our lessons and move on. When you resist a lesson, life will repeat the lesson until you get it. How do you get the lesson? Become aware of it, change your perspective, and make a different choice. For example, if you keep dating alcoholics or addicts, maybe try choosing a mate who doesn't drink or take drugs or abstain from alcohol yourself because maybe that's the lesson you need to learn.

As we go through these life lessons, we often get caught up in them. That is to say we get caught up in the drama. It's as if you're a piece of driftwood being tossed side to side by a strong current. Then we go through strong emotions as each day passes depending on what happens. As a result, we can't seem to find stillness. In addition our egos feed off the drama and perpetuate it. Consequently we get sucked into a victim mindset and relinquish our control to people and situations. A major part of the twin flame journey is learning to transcend the ego and ego-based consciousness.

The World of Ego

We live in a world that caters to the ego and its desires. Separately there is nothing wrong with desires or the ego. I teach according to the philosophy of Vedanta and the yoga sutras of Patanjali combined which state that ego is not a thing to be killed or scorned. The ego is part of who you are. It helps define your personality and boundaries on this earth plane. In fact, you must embrace the ego in order to transcend it. Your ego will help you be in healthy relationships and accept the conditionality of human existence. Yet your ego can easily be the most constricted part of who you are.

Societal conditioning is largely based on satisfaction of the ego in what I like to call the survival mode of the first three chakras. The base chakra, sacral chakra, and the solar plexus chakra all have to do with getting basic physical and emotional needs met as well as seeking out power in the world. Again I emphasize, nothing is inherently wrong with getting needs met. We all have needs and they must be met. But if you go through your entire life only focused on these physical aspects, you tend to deal with a lot of garbage.

As spiritual beings having a human experience, we are designed for so much more. When we're caught up in the cycle of going to school or work, paying the bills, running errands, seeking out control in relationships, and fighting for justice, we're never ascending to higher levels of being. Most of the forms of entertainment reflect this mentality. All you need to do is look at the popularity of dramatic talk and reality shows to see what most people are focused on.

Now you might now be wondering if *you* have issues with your ego. To find out, you can take an ego inventory by looking for certain behavioral traits. A good indication of ego consciousness is living in fear or being ruled by fear and anxiety, having arguments with others to "prove a point", getting on the defensive often, and having control issues. Moreover, the ego is constantly searching for confirmation and affirmation. It wants the pat on the back and waits for the other to say, "Job well done!"

We all have shadows of our egos. That being said, the way to address those shadows is to move toward them to take a look and not run away from them. One time I had to be at a dinner with my twin. It was a professional setting so I could barely look at him. At the dinner was this woman, a colleague, who was hanging all over him most of the night. Talk about an ego flareup! My ego flared up so big that I got angry, upset, and frustrated all at the same time. Inside my head I was screaming at her, "Get your hands off of him. He's mine!" Oh yes, and that's the ego's mantra, "That's mine!" After the dinner was over, I cried all the way home. When I got home I was ready to throw in the towel. *That's it!* I told myself, *He doesn't love me or want to be with me. He wants to be with her. I should just give up now.* Then I stopped and thought more rationally. *What is it in me that's causing me to react in this way? Did he seem to be into her? Or did he seem uncomfortable too?* The more questions I asked, the calmer I became. In other words, I had to find the ego trigger and once I found it, I was able to see things differently. Ultimately, I was frustrated that we couldn't be together in public, talk to one another, or even be friends. Because of what we really felt for each other, any display of even friendship would be too transparent. In addition I was jealous and angry that another female colleague could give him hugs and put her arm around him, without any eyebrows raising in suspicion, because they had no true connection. As you can see by my example, ego always wreaks havoc on your sense of peace.

Taming the Ego

Getting the ego to become your servant and not the other way around is an uphill battle in the beginning. Throughout my life, I suffered from an underlying sense of anxiety. Most of the anxiety was due to my upbringing and not being able to trust the people who raised me. Some of it came from my educational and religious upbringing. And yet what remained was either inborn personality traits or past life experiences. Growing up I was afraid of many things most of the time. Yet, oddly enough I took risks and lunged at experiences that continually took me out of my comfort zone. In hindsight, I believe that was part of my spiritual training. However, it wasn't until I had my experience with cancer at age twenty-eight that I was shoved into a corner where I had to confront my ego.

For the duration of that life-changing experience I was faced with all of my fears at once. I saw the fear of dying, the fear of not being able to be alive for my small children, the fear of my marital relationship not being what I wanted, the fear of my parents not being there for me, and the fear of going mentally insane. All of those things were thrust to the forefront of my life and spread out in front of me to face head on. By far it was the darkest period of my life. When I was in it, I never thought I could get out of it. But the whole time God was present, holding my hand, and leading me through the darkness. During those painful two to three years, I picked up yoga again and learned mindfulness guided meditation. I began studying methods of natural healing and reading about spiritual philosophies. At that time I had to learn to control my mind and ego or I would have gone insane. The pressure was simply too intense for me to handle alone. I had to put my faith in God and let go. In addition, I had to awaken to the fact that I had direct control over my mind and ego.

The only way to transcend the confines of the ego is to connect with your higher spiritual self and to operate from that aspect of you. As you learn to do this more and more, you will no longer see yourself through the lens of the ego.

The Journey Within

All of this work is designed to force you to go deep within. Many who begin the twin flame journey feel like most of us when we encounter problems. We look outside of ourselves for answers. In the beginning this can be helpful. When you're unfamiliar with a topic or situation, getting a point of reference can be educational and comforting. But after that, it's important to turn inward to your own experiences and intuition.

More than many life experiences, the twin flame one pushes, pulls, and prods until we must go within. No matter how much you fight it, you will find yourself at this point. God wants you to trust and he wants you to do his work. And you can't do that if you're still searching for outside answers. Here's why. Most people don't possess the spiritual awareness to trust their inner knowing. They have to gather facts, data, and opinions in order to make a decision about their own lives. Herein lies the problem. No one can know the extent of your personal story except for you and God. No one knows your life plan and purpose but you and God. I don't care if they're the best psychic or spiritual teacher in the world. No one can claim to know your entire story. And I say this as a psychic and spiritual teacher.

The Work: How You Transform

The reason is because God *is* God. He is omniscient and omnipotent. As human beings, God can and does give us gifts including clairvoyance. But the way my teachers explained it to me and the way I see it in my readings with others is that God will give you a few of the puzzle pieces as a reader but not all the pieces. He may give other pieces to other readers. But you will never, ever see the entire picture. Therefore, spiritually enlightened people can give you guidance to help you move forward on your journey. But only you truly know where and how to go.

The one major question I get as a YouTuber on twin flame forums and with my clients is, "How do I know if this person is my twin flame?" The answer is that you just know. When you are in tune with yourself and your intuition, you simply know. That doesn't mean there won't be moments of doubt. In fact you will frequently have doubts, especially in the beginning. But the underlying feeling is that you will know. You feel your twin inside of you. Your twin is an integral part of who you are. The pain in separation from your twin is unmatched to any other separation.

My twin and I were in a situation where we couldn't be together or even look at each other. We knew our situation was difficult, but we didn't realize how difficult it was until something major happened. After that point the external separation got even more pronounced than it was before. He couldn't talk to me, look at me, or smile at me. If anyone suspected anything of our connection it could have had serious implications. It was also at that point that I came to a harsh realization of what I needed to do. I had some inklings of what I had to do brewing beneath the surface. But I wasn't in a hurry to make the changes I knew in my heart I needed to make. Now if I had asked anyone's opinion, who was not on the twin flame journey, they would have said I was completely insane. They would have told me I was taking huge risks. They would have told me I was stupid for letting go of something so good and stable. And they would have pointed out the reasons why I shouldn't make those changes including a laundry list of all of my past failures. Believe me, I've heard it all in the past and also in my own head by my own inner critic. (Your inner critic can be very loud. :)) Yet in my heart, I knew I had to make those changes. First of all, separation from my twin became unbearable. It was bad before the incident but much worse after it. By me choosing to change a situation that was in my power to change, I could alleviate the pressure and tension keeping us apart. But it did require great faith and a tremendous amount of trust in God and my intuition.

Usually a leap of faith and trust in your inner voice requires diving into the unknown. Most people don't have the spiritual tenacity to be able to handle the unknown. Those of us who are able to go within and move forward from that place eventually become accustomed

The Work: How You Transform

to diving into the depths of the unknown. Though it doesn't make it more comfortable. (As I wrote this, I looked at my phone and it read 11:11. That's my Angels confirming the truth of this section. :))

In our society we're not taught to go within. Meditation is a relatively new teaching in the Western world and not everyone accepts it. I've even heard extreme religious groups scorn meditation by saying, "An idle mind is the devil's playground." Yet silence is God's one and only true voice. If you don't get silent, you won't get to appreciate the fullness of God and hear his messages. In the next chapter I'll outline ways in which you can get in touch with your inner wisdom more readily.

8

Homework for Spiritual Growth

*M*ANY OF US ON the twin flame path underestimate the amount of work *we* have to do. It's too easy to "assign" homework to our twin, whether expressly or in the 5D. Because you generally see everything about your twin flame, you see clearly all of the work that they need to do to get ready for reunion. Please note (and underline *and* highlight the following); it is NONE of your business to decide what your twin flame has to do to get ready to be with you. That is God's business and not yours. Your only business is determining what *you* must do to get your life in order in every way to prepare yourself for reunion. Following your path is the only thing you can do.

In other words, your twin might take the most convoluted pathway to get to you. He might stop by a pub in Ireland, grab a few drinks, then take a few years to climb Mount Everest, go back to the pub in Ireland only to make his way to South Africa to pet some penguins. Whatever he does is none of your business. Eventually your twin flame *will* get to you. That is his destiny. And the more you complain about your twin and the fact that they're not doing what you think they need to do to get on *your* path, the more you will delay things.

Homework #1: Take Care of Your Body

Your body is the temple housing your soul and your twin flame's soul. It's your job to honor your body by feeding it whole foods and pure water. It's also your job to exercise it, give it rest, and stretch it when needed. In addition, you must keep toxic substances away from your body including alcohol, tobacco, or any other type of drug.

The twin flame journey is hardcore. You can't expect to ascend to higher states of consciousness if your body is bogged down with toxins. Nor can you expect to have a smooth reunion if you've been ignoring your body because you're too wrapped up in trying to get your twin to be with you.

Many people don't like hearing this message. They think that one thing has nothing to do with the other. You might find you've created some resistance around getting healthy. Furthermore, you might also notice that you've been too focused on how your twin is acting and any lifestyle flaws they might have. That is one slippery slope you don't want to get onto. Focus on you and your health. Your twin will have to be concerned with theirs.

I've written three books to help you start living a healthy lifestyle if it's been difficult for you:

The Wheel of Healing with Ayurveda: An Easy Guide to a Healthy Lifestyle

Enlightened Medicine Your Power to Get Well Now: An Integrative Approach to Healing the 7 Deadly Lifestyle Diseases

Chakra Healing for Vibrant Energy: Exploring your 7 Energy Centers with Mindfulness, Yoga, and Ayurveda

Even if you have a lot of changes to make, try not to make all the changes at once. It will be overwhelming and you will probably give up after a short while. Perhaps you can try integrating one change per month or every couple of weeks. The great benefit of spiritual awakening is that you start to intuitively know what's good for your body. Just follow your body's wisdom and you will know what to do to make your body feel strong.

Homework #2: Meditate

Meditation is essential for healthy living. To ascend to higher spiritual planes it's also a must. Find a good meditation teacher and learn how to meditate. Once you learn, practice it daily. It will calm the monkey mind.

Additionally, it will make this twin flame journey feel less crazy. The more you meditate, the stronger your intuition will become. The reason for this is that meditation helps to align you with the flow of the universe. When you align with the flow, you're less likely to fight experiences that come your way.

Meditating helps take you beyond the confines of your ego. By the same token, when you meditate daily you lower the number of thoughts that flit about in your mind. Most people believe that they have no control over their thoughts. With this belief, thoughts become scary and unpredictable. This is especially true for those who suffer from anxiety disorders or depression. If you suffer from one or the other, you know that racing thoughts often lead to panic attacks or a deeper depressive state. Through your meditation practice, not only do you lower the number of thoughts in a day, but also your thoughts become more organized.

In like manner, you can practice silence and mindfulness so that you can become accustomed to sitting in stillness. As a whole, we're not used to sitting in quiet-stillness and that in and of itself can produce anxiety. But the more you turn off the TV or music or silence your phone, the more your mind will learn to accept your new tranquil reality. In the beginning meditation can seem like a lot to swallow because being faced with your thoughts might be an unwelcome reality. You might be thinking, *That's why I keep so busy. I don't want to know what's in there.* Well, the sooner you confront what's in your mind, the better you'll feel once all of your emotional clutter is seen in full view. And as I always mention in all of my books recommending meditation, seek help from a professional therapist if emotions and thoughts get too intense for you to handle on your own. Emotional detox can sometimes be more difficult than a body detox. Therefore, embrace your inner strength by seeking help when you need it. Furthermore, if you're taking any psychotropic prescription medications (mental health prescriptions), do not, under any circumstance, stop taking them without the help of a medical professional even if you find that meditation is working wonders for your mental health. If you're uncertain as to whether or not your psychiatrist would be on board with alternative health practices, you can always seek an integrative health care specialist so you can meld conventional Western medicine with other methods such as meditation under supervised care.

In addition to all of the health benefits of meditation, it also helps you connect better in the 5D with your twin. Just as biological twins can communicate telepathically and non-verbally, when you move beyond your mind, intellect, and ego, you'll start to "feel" messages from your twin. During the separation phase, communication that goes beyond the traditional methods can be a comfort in order to feel that you're still connected.

At my live events I offer an introduction to meditation and I also conduct online meditation classes.

Homework #3: Let Go of Control

The main reason many of us are caught up in a vicious cycle of repeating the same life lessons is that we have a hard time letting go of control. Remember that seeking control or trying to remain in control is a major ego issue. The ego wants to rule the roost and is going to make you believe that by taking control, you're going to get what you want. In fact, the opposite is true. The more you let go and let God, the faster you'll obtain what you desire including reunion with your twin.

Keep in mind that the need to control comes from a place of fear. The fearful part of you says, *I don't have enough. I don't feel safe. I'm not worthy to receive.* When you're full of fear, it's based on lack of faith in God. In the Bible, God tells us over a hundred times not to be afraid or to not fear. In other words, God is in control so you don't have to be. The truthful realization upon awakening is that you were never in control in the first place.

So what does it mean to let go of control? It means you run your race and let others do the same. Be loving, kind, generous, patient, and forgiving but stay out of the compulsion to be a puppet master for other people's lives. For many people this is a very difficult thing to do.

When it comes to romantic relationships, most people try to manipulate and control the other person. Somehow they equate love to telling the other person what to do and how to live their life. Then they justify their words and actions by saying, "I'm just being loving. If I see something they're doing wrong, it's only because I love them that I must say something." Herein lies the problem with that logic. When you give your opinion as to how someone else has to live their lives, you're taking away their freewill choice to live as they choose. In trying to get them to live how you believe is the right way, you're not only telling them that they're wrong and you're right, but you're also derailing them from their path and forcing them onto yours.

For example, when I was in a relationship with an alcoholic, in the beginning I would throw away his alcohol. I thought I was doing him a favor. Firstly, he got irate. Secondly, I learned that by throwing the alcohol away I was doing *him* a disservice. Here's why. In a recovery group I learned that by throwing away his alcohol I was actually preventing him from getting sober. Most of the time alcoholics have to hit rock bottom on their own. And by manipulating the situation, I was not only taking away his freewill choice to drink, but also I was perhaps removing the drink that might make him hit his bottom. Who's to say? By taking away the alcohol, I was trying to play God.

Understandably, in relationships you will find things that bother you and your partner will find things that bother them about you. But those things are better worked out in compromise and discussion. As you reach a place of unconditional love, you're better able to come to those compromises without manipulation, threats, insults, and control games.

Homework #4: Release Co-Dependent Relationships

As you progress to a much higher spiritual plane, you will begin to release relationships that are co-dependent in nature. Unfortunately most relationships operate on some level of co-dependency. And that's because a majority of the human population is very much rooted in the physical plane. When you're operating from the first three chakras, for the most part, you're going to get a lot of crap when interacting with people.

If you're not familiar with the chakras, they're a good reference point for understanding human psyche and the progression of spiritual development. My book, *Chakra Healing for Vibrant Energy,* gives a simple yet profound explanation of the chakras. But here's a miniexplanation of the first three chakras to help you understand why human relationships are so darn complicated.

The first chakra, or the root, deals with having your basic needs met. It's the survival chakra. The needs to seek shelter, find food, get money, and provide for your

Homework for Spiritual Growth

loved ones on a basic level are all rooted in this chakra. Fears mostly stem from this chakra being out of balance. The second chakra is the chakra of creativity and procreation. It's called the sacral or sexual chakra. You can look at the second chakra as one of sensual pleasures. The third chakra is the personal power chakra or to put it in more tangible terms, the ego chakra. It's about going out into the world, proving who you are, and getting what you want for yourself. Inherently, nothing is wrong with any of these chakras. They are a part of human existence. We need these energies to live here. However, if you limit yourself to these three energetic sources, you will be limited as a person. If we were to sum up the first three chakras with three mantras they would be:

I need to survive.

I need to procreate.

I need what's mine.

Do you see how these mantras can create a sense of desperation and angst? Now imagine that two people are coming together whilst living rooted in the first three chakras, with those same mantras, and trying to make a relationship work. Can you see the impending disaster at hand?

To further this illustration, if I need to survive and you need to survive, who's needs come first? And if I need to procreate, but you don't want to procreate, then someone else convinces you to procreate, what happens then? Finally, we all know what happens when I'm trying to take what's mine and you're claiming what's yours. To see that, all you need to do is observe kids in a school playground or employees in a large corporation.

Co-dependency is an unhealthy dynamic dance of two people being dishonest and manipulating one another to get what they both want. And if you don't think you do this, honestly observe yourself in relationships. We *all* have done this.

Have you ever been a people-pleaser? People-pleasing is one of the most dishonest relationship behaviors that exists. You give in to what you *think* the other person wants or you actually give in to what the person says they want. And you only do it to show you're accommodating or the better person. First of all, it's deceiving to underhandedly establish superiority and boost your own ego. Secondly, it's a lie to deny your own feelings, wants, and desires by pretending they don't exist. In the end you're lying to yourself and to the other person. Lastly, people-pleasing creates animosity, anger, and passive-aggressive behavior that comes from the person who gave in to people-please. Because you've ignored your truth and truthful feelings to "give up" to the other person, you feel that they somehow owe you for giving up what you truly wanted. Do you see how toxic that behavior is? But you smooth it over by saying that you're a "nice" person. And that is a co-dependent behavior.

You can release and change co-dependent relationships by first getting honest with yourself and the other person. Get honest about what you're willing to tolerate and not tolerate. If you find things you can't tolerate and those are the same things, which the other person is not willing to change, then make the decision to leave or stay. But do it consciously. If you decide to stay in it, learn to accept the behavior as something you can't change in another. And you if you decide to leave the relationship, make sure you've learned so as to not attract the same relationship in another person. Inversely, if you feel that the other person is asking *you* to do things that push you outside of your moral parameters, then it's up to you to put your foot down and say no.

And that brings us to the next item on your homework list, setting healthy boundaries.

Homework #5 Create Healthy Boundaries

A fallacy exists in religious and spiritual circles, and that is, you must be selfless and give at 100% or you're not a spiritual person. Therefore, as lightworkers and empaths we take those teachings to heart and become even more selfless than we are already hardwired to be. For those of us who come into the world to give, we don't need more teachings encouraging us to give *more*, we need teachings that encourage us to hold back a little bit. And that is where this teaching will seem very backward to you.

As a lightworker, you remember a place that has no boundaries. Spirit is timeless, spaceless, and boundless. You remember infinite love and acceptance. Then you come into this world and try to practice these spiritual concepts by living them. As a result you hit a roadblock when people take advantage of you and walk all over you like an area rug. Then you wonder what you did wrong. What you did wrong was that you were living by heaven's principles and not Earth's principles. In order to live on Earth, you need a balance of living in the spaceless, boundless existence of spirit *and* in the confining boundaries of Earth.

The problem with most lightworkers is that living with healthy boundaries does not feel good at all. It feels selfish and unnatural. Thus, most lightworkers revert back to living by spiritual principles while dealing with first-three-chakra beings and then feel sad and wronged when they get hurt, yet again.

Let me say this to you with the utmost love and compassion. *You need healthy boundaries.* Learning how to create boundaries is part of your work here and also part of the twin flame journey. It took me many years to be able to create healthy boundaries and it's still an uphill journey for me.

And if you think I'm spiritual, you haven't met my twin. I always say that he is a *much* better person than me. He is by far the most loving, giving, compassionate, and understanding person I've ever met. But he has had to work through issues with boundary setting too. In fact, the more spiritual you are naturally, the harder you'll have to work at setting boundaries.

The problem is that those without healthy boundaries have no idea how to create them. Many good books exist to help you with this task. Two of my favorite books are *Boundaries* and *Safe People* by Drs. Henry Cloud and John Townsend. But even before you're able to read other books, a simple way to start is by making a list of what you're willing to accept and not accept in your life.

For example, if you only want honest people in your immediate circle, stay away from those who are dishonest. If you want sober people in your life, stay away from bars, pubs, and clubs where people drink. Or if you don't like having out of town guests stay with you when visiting, get the names and numbers of a few good Air B&Bs in your neighborhood or some reasonably priced hotels.

When it comes to your twin flame, boundary setting is important too. Many believe that because their twin is their one and only true love that they can't set boundaries with them. Nothing could be further from the truth. Boundary setting is about respecting yourself. For example, if your twin consistently calls you after 11 p.m. and you prefer to be sleeping at that hour, ask them to call before or in the morning and then tell them you're setting your phone to "do not disturb" mode. It might sound like a ridiculous example, but I'll bet you can think back to all of the things you've done for people in the past to bend over backward to accommodate them, while ignoring your own needs.

Finally, it's important to respect other people's boundaries. Even though you would bend over backwards to get someone else's needs met, that doesn't mean that the person in question wants to do the same. One of the lessons you'll learn in accepting that you need boundaries is to more readily accept others' boundaries, even if it doesn't give you what you need. (Please, for your own sanity, highlight and underline what follows. :)) Respecting others' boundaries includes your twin flame's boundaries. When he or she says that they need their space and that they can't talk to you or be with you, respect that. If your twin says that they never want to see you again, respect that. None of the extreme boundary setting with your twin will probably last for very long, but nonetheless, you must respect them just as much as anyone else will respect yours. Remember, unconditional love means unconditionally loving the boundaries your twin sets for you and for them.

Homework: #6 Move Toward Non-Judgment

Back in 2010 I did a silent meditation retreat with Deepak Chopra. The funny thing is that it wasn't even a total silent retreat. Out of 300 participants, about 30 of us opted to do three days of silence with special teachings.

Homework for Spiritual Growth

The general teachings were still in the large room with all of the other participants who weren't silent. To set this story up properly, I must tell you that I didn't really want to do the silent bit. I had finished all of the Chopra Center certifications by October 2009 and had been teaching yoga, Ayurveda, and meditation since mid-2008. A friend and fellow Chopra Center teacher had encouraged me to do the silent retreat by telling me it would be life-changing. In retrospect, I was not mentally ready for that type of mind challenge. Imagine, sitting in silence for a thirty-minute meditation is a challenge for most people. Now extend thirty minutes to three days or 72 hours. That meant no talking, texting, or typing anything to anyone for that amount of time. During that retreat I learned quickly what your mind does when you give it that latitude. When you first become silent your mind becomes very loud. It will take the opportunity to say many things to you. Then it will quiet down, but afterward emotions start to come up. And boy did they come up. About the second day I had an emotional breakdown that required me to talk a little just to reassure others that I was okay. But that's not even what shocked me the most. The most shocking piece of those silent three days was that I realized how judgmental I was. That's right, in my silence I began judging people. This surprised me because in my waking and talking life, I feel that I'm a pretty accepting person. But getting me silent in 2010, made me see a whole new side to myself. People who I didn't even know began to irritate me. I thought to myself, *Wow, I'm a really awful person. I judge people a lot.*

Given that example I'm able to diffuse a sensitive topic by pointing out my flaws first. And I would hope that I've grown a lot since then. However I think it's safe to say that to some extent we are all judgmental.

When you judge another, you disregard them. Furthermore, a judgment is an assessment that may or may not be true. The ego wants to judge to point out its superiority or to deflect from itself. Those who judge the most have deep-seated insecurities.

The more you judge your twin, the more you alienate them. In the beginning of our separation, I was angry with my twin for letting go of a great connection. I knew he was afraid, but I judged him for being blind to his own feelings. Somehow it made me feel better that I could judge him at the time. But then it just made me feel worse because I knew I couldn't do anything about the fact that he was afraid. No matter how much I loved him, he had to figure out how *he* felt about me. As the layers of my own fears and insecurities began to get uncovered, I discovered that throughout my life I too had pushed people away when they got too close. In the end, I realized that I was pointing the finger at him, but in fact I had the exact same issue that was also pushing him away.

As you begin to practice non-judgment, know that discernment is not the same as judgment. Discernment is necessary to live a healthy life. For example, if your favorite cousin is a heroin addict and you believe he shouldn't be around you, that's good discernment. Saying he's a horrible person for it, is a judgment. Do you see the difference? He might be sick with an addiction, but underneath he's still a child of God.

Know that practicing non-judgment is a very hard thing to do. Cut yourself some slack in the beginning. And a great tool to combat judgment is practicing gratitude.

Homework #7 Practice Gratitude

It is nearly impossible to judge *and* practice authentic gratitude at the same time. When you are in the attitude of being grateful it cancels out judgment. In the twin flame journey, staying rooted in gratitude can be complicated. Nevertheless, it can be a cure-all to seeing the glass as half empty. Hundreds of times during our separation I couldn't understand why certain things were happening. It was so painful not to see him or be able to talk to him. At times I had to actively work at what I was grateful for. In fact, even though it was torture at times, I was grateful that I got to see my twin regularly even though we couldn't talk or share our lives together.

Practicing gratitude is not only essential in the twin flame journey, but it's also an important practice in daily living. Focusing on what you're grateful for will bring you more abundance and happiness. For some it doesn't come naturally. But it's definitely a muscle you can build over time.

Homework #8: Moving Toward Inter-Dependency

The one major problem lightworkers and empaths have is going from co-dependency in relationships to isolation. Since they have heightened sensitivity to others, it's easy for them to try and take on the world to be the world's savior. Meanwhile they forget that other people exist who can help them in their passionate endeavors. In addition to the martyr or victim mentality of, *Oh well, no one else is going to help, I might as well do it myself*, lightworkers also have issues with money. Money is an earthly concept and those of us who live in the ethers can have difficulty accepting it as being necessary for our journey here. Therefore, many lightworkers will not charge enough for their products and services, take on jobs that don't pay well, or give away too much of their money in an effort to *help* others.

The lack of abundance is doubled by the mindset that people can't be trusted. As a lightworker, you have the innocence of seeing the good in people, and when people let you down, you are shocked each and every time. This realization erodes your faith in humanity and further reinforces the mentality of having to do it all alone.

A major step in moving toward an enlightened life and also toward your twin flame is accepting that, as humans, we are interdependent beings and that's the way we are created. By believing you have to do it all yourself shows that you're missing the point. God wants us to be able to rely on each other and share the burden. He doesn't want us to live in isolation. From the time we take our first breath on Earth, we're designed to bond with others. To emphasize this point, a newborn placed on her mother's chest will move her way up to the breast to seek nourishment and sustenance. This example shows that it's God's will for us to not live in isolation; otherwise he never would have created us to be reliant on one another for survival.

Even through adversity, in relationship we become the best version of who we are. Yet in isolation we become self-centered and our worldview becomes skewed. Your relationship with your twin is designed to help you create healthy interdependence. Through many of my meditations concerning my twin flame, I had strong awakenings about this topic. Starting with my parents, many of my relationships left me with an inability to trust. Therefore, I had always held back who I am for fear that I would be burned. Because of the cruel backlashes of those who I thought loved me, I would hold back affection, information, time, or money from the people in my life. With the exception of my children, no one else was able to see me completely for who I am. Earlier I gave the example of how I made an agreement with God not to withhold anything from my twin. Once I agreed to give everything I have and everything I am to my twin, I felt totally at peace. I know now that my twin is the first person in my life (besides my children) whom I can trust completely and that he will never take advantage of me like others have. Do you realize how liberating that is? When you know you can be completely interdependent on another person and that you don't have to do it all alone, it's the best feeling in the world. And that is what God wants to teach you through your journey with your twin flame. Yet it's only through the power of self-love that you'll be able to stay open to the experience of trusting another completely. Let's explore what it will take to be able to attract the full spectrum of unconditional love into your energy field.

Homework #9: Anchor the Light

The early stages of a twin flame union can be completely ungrounding. Therefore, it's important that you ground yourself. Eat grounding foods such as potatoes and other root vegetables. Practice meditation on the earth where you can feel nature underneath you. Imagine roots coming out of your bottom and anchoring you to Mother Earth.

Homework for Spiritual Growth

During the journey to twin flame reunion, you will sense your inner light coming through. You might feel glowing or floating. Now is the time to anchor that light by remaining in your body while allowing your soul to transcend. This is easier said than done. Since feeling the connection to your twin in the 5D is pleasurable, you may be tempted to stay in that experience and not embrace living. If you're flitting about most of the time in the Angelic realm having out of body experiences, your light is not necessarily benefitting the rest of humanity. Therefore, help the collectivity by remaining in balance. Stay grounded and live in the present moment. Instead of spreading your light upward back toward heaven; begin to spread it outward over the earth by serving others with your gifts and talents.

As you ascend into higher states of awareness, many of these homework assignments won't seem like work at all. They will begin to come naturally. The best part about the twin flame journey is that because you and your twin are soul-connected, when you work on yourself, your twin will see changes in him or herself too. So while you can't change your twin and of course you wouldn't want to, they will receive soul upgrades by your work.

9

The Liberation of Self-Love

*D*URING THE COURSE OF the twin flame journey we are so focused on our twin that we can lose sight of loving ourselves. Most of the time, we stay in worry energy because we crave love from our twin. We worry about whether or not they love us back or are even awakened to the connection. That worry carries us away from providing the love we must give to ourselves.

I know I see my twin as a divine being of light. When I look into his eyes I find I'm home. The love I experience when I look at him is the same as the love I experienced with God before I came. During most of our separation, I was under the belief that I could only experience that oneness by looking into his eyes. But then

I realized that I could give myself that same love by feeling the complete love of God the Father. Furthermore, the mirroring of love I am so willing to give to my twin can also be reflected back to me.

Since God is love and the ultimate creator, you, as a being of light also have the gift to create. Many twin flames remain in separation because they doubt their power to manifest. Once you have raised your vibrational frequency to the level of unconditional love in every aspect of being, your natural ability is to create.

You Are a Co-Creator of Your Own Destiny

God would have never put the promise in your heart if it weren't meant to come to pass. Your desire to be with your twin is written in God's plan. He would have never put your twin flame in your heart or in your physical space if you weren't meant to be together. Many who enter this twin flame journey choose to stay in separation because they lack faith. They remain in doubt and stay involved in self-destructing behaviors. Other times they get impatient and abandon the journey. God is always going to give you a freewill choice to be in 3D union or to stay in separation. And remember, nothing is a surprise to God. In the end, God has always known what you will do and the choices you will make.

Like most twin flame romantic journeys, mine was not an easy one. Many huge obstacles stood in the way of my twin flame and I. On the surface it seemed that

The Liberation of Self-Love

there was not a single reason why we should be together. In the beginning I couldn't understand why God chose him for me. The man I thought was for me seemed to be a perfect match. We were around the same age, had a great relationship, our personalities meshed almost perfectly, our beliefs were similar, and we were crazy in love with one another. Yet, the rift that existed between us seemed to be ever-present. God held me back. And I never understood why until I met my twin. A few days after I met my twin, God told me that he was meant for me.

Furthermore, God told me, through my Angels, that he had created my twin specifically for me. God's message was clear: *There exists no other perfect match for me or for him.* Even thought I couldn't see it in the beginning, God let me see his glory. Every time I talked to my twin, usually in a time of crisis, this man revealed himself to me. And each time God showed me, who my twin was on the inside, I saw how perfect he was for me. Every word, every anecdote, and every look filled my soul with what it needed.

Here's the thing, even before my twin began to reveal to me who he is, I got into agreement with God. Oh I argued with God, for about an hour. But after that, I said to God, "Thy will be done." I know not to fight with God and his will. I surrendered to him in saying, "Okay God, if you say that this man is the right one for me, I'll obey you. I trust you. I believe you and I will do your will and not mine."

That's when the shit hit the fan. Instead of having a perfect journey with my twin we ran into some brick walls. For example, I imagined my twin and I running through a flower-filled meadow in romantic bliss, but that's not the way it went down. If you've ever read the Bible, God tends to teach lessons that way. He says, "Okay. We're going to do things my way now. I'm going to give you a crapload of stuff to deal with and you're going to have to trust me." For this reason, you must have the spiritual backbone to endure such challenges along the twin flame journey.

You are a co-creator *with* God. Most of the time, God is not going to hand you what you want on a silver platter. If he did you wouldn't appreciate it or learn the lessons you are intended to learn through the process. It's often this refusal of process that gets us into trouble.

The Power of a Decision

The etymology of the word *decision* comes from the Latin past-participle of *decidere* which means "to decide, to determine" or literally "to cut off from". When you make a decision, you are cutting off other options. You are telling God and the universe, "This is what I want." It requires great strength to make some decisions. Cutting off other options isn't always easy. In the age of immediate gratification the mantra is more like, "I'm keeping my options open." The problem with keeping options open is that you're constantly sending mixed signals to the universe. When you want to manifest a desired outcome, the universe can't provide it if you're saying, "I want *this* but also *that*," when the two options are in direct conflict with one another.

Many of the ones I've heard are:
- I want to be with my twin flame but I don't want to leave my marriage.
- I *want* this to work but she lives 3,000 miles from me.
- We work together and a relationship in the workplace is frowned upon. But I can't quit my job.
- What if I change my situation for my twin flame and it doesn't work out?
- My twin flame is a lot younger than me so we can't be in a relationship but I want to be.
- We are from different religions or cultures and my family would disown me if I marry my twin flame and I don't want to abandon my family.
- I want to be with my twin but if I leave my current situation I may not be okay financially.

Do you understand now how you can be sending a completely conflictual message to the universe and God based on your belief systems? Most right decisions are never easy to make. But the hard decisions are often the right ones.

Focus on Your Desired Outcome

As I began writing today, I asked my twin in the 5D, "What should I write about today?" And his higher self answered me, "Write about my commitment to you." That made me cry because in the darkest of times during separation, I couldn't tell if he even cared about me, let alone if he was committed to me. Nevertheless, I had to hold onto the belief that he was indeed committed to me. I had to believe it with every fiber of my being. To me, my twin is the most beautiful soul that exists on the planet. Being without him was never on the table. And his commitment to me is only reflective of my commitment to him, even before reunion.

During our separation I had to remain steadfast in my belief every second, minute, and hour of every day that we would reunite. I was so incredibly committed to my belief in our return to each other that I would envision it daily. Moreover, I would write to his higher self every single day as if we were lovers separated by distance in medieval times with only a horse and messenger to deliver the letters. In every daydream and vision, I could smell him, taste him, experience him, and hear his voice. Furthermore, I knew, beyond all shadow of any doubt that we would be together forever. It's that kind of commitment that gets you to reunion.

Stay in Faith

Once you have your desired outcome in mind, all you need to do is have faith that it will come to fruition. God doesn't need you to manipulate or control it into being. He doesn't need you to perform tricks or create love potions.

One of the biggest comments I see on my YouTube channel is, "I think I did something to mess things up with my twin flame." That is the biggest heap of nonsense I've ever heard. You can't do anything to mess things up completely with your twin. God is too big for that. You can, however, delay things a bit or momentarily take a different path for a while. But hear me as I say this; you can never, ever, in a billion years mess up God's plan for you and your twin.

Reunion with your twin might come faster when you have unshakable faith. And here is the best part; you don't have to do anything. Sit back and let God orchestrate the events that will bring you and your twin together. Instead of actively pushing and prodding to get your twin to be with you, notice the signs, messages, and coincidences. The more you pay attention, the more ready you'll be to act when the time is right.

My Angels and guides knew when I was struggling and helped me to stay in faith. During those times they would send me signs around the clock. For example, I have two ceiling lights in my bathroom that, depending on the shadows, reflect as two rings meeting and crossing at the center like wedding bands. When I would doubt my twin's and my connection, the light hit just right so I would see those rings. Another time, as I felt my faith faltering, I walked into a grocery store and in front of me was a card that read, "Happy Wedding!" Each time I saw those and other signs, I heard, *Michelle, he's your guy. You two are going to be married. Don't worry. Stay in faith.*

The Return to Self-Love

As someone who loves and has a desire to love, it can be difficult to give yourself love. Oftentimes we believe that loving ourselves is someone else's job. As a result, we sit around and wait for that magical moment when another person pops up to love us. Or even worse we go around chasing love. Like a butterfly seeking nectar from a field of wildflowers, we flit from person to person with the expectation that we *must* find someone to love us. And while we're out there, we're trying to fill a void. Then we stand surprised when no one returns our love or when that magical person doesn't show up on our doorstep.

In all relationships, the best way to enter into them is when you're filled with self-love. But for a twin flame relationship, it's a must. A huge part of your learning experience is about the discovery of self-love. You and your twin are not coming together to fill a void but rath-

The Liberation of Self-Love

er to enhance the experience of each other's lives, which will enable you to expand outward into the world.

In love relationships, I had spent my entire life trying to find a romantic partner to fill a void. I needed a man or I needed a relationship. And I needed someone to love me. Meeting my twin made me realize that all of my searching was based on fear because I didn't have faith in the love I could give myself. My twin flame is the perfect man for me in every way. But he is also a perfect person on his own. He doesn't need me to complete him or to fill a void inside. He is an amazingly complete man with or without me. Because he loves me and I love him, we want to be together. Besides it being written in our divine life purpose, we also *choose* to be with each other.

During our separation I had some difficult lessons to learn about self-love. I had fears about being alone or being single. Early in life I equated being single to being in pain. To me it meant not being loved enough to have a man love me. And to me that was extremely painful. Therefore, imagine the pain I was in when my twin didn't want to be with me. It was pure torture. I knew he loved and cared about me, yet he didn't want to be with me. What a cruel twist of fate right? But in his subconscious inner wisdom he knew he needed to give me the space to learn how to love myself completely. The truth is, he could have opted to stay with me, love me completely, and be the perfect boyfriend. But because I couldn't receive self-love to the intensity at which he could bring me love, I wouldn't have believed it or received it. At that time I would have consistently doubted his love for me.

Finally, about eight months into our separation, I came to a point at which I could accept and love myself regardless of my relationship status. I could be happy, fulfilled, and joyful whether or not my twin was with me. For me, that was huge. In my entire life, I don't ever remember feeling completely full and satisfied unless I had a man reflecting back to me how much he loved me. During that time I had taken a trip by myself to Mexico. Everyone I met at the resort was dumbfounded that a pretty lady such as myself should travel alone. A few days into my stay, a woman I had been chatting with said to me, "Isn't a part of you just a little pissed that you're here alone?" And I could respond in all honesty, "No. I'm actually good." The truth is, I was good. I was great, in fact. The old me would have been having a pity party, but the new Michelle, filled with self-love, felt totally at peace. The best part is, my newly found sense of self-love was established during the separation from my twin. The love of my life gave me that gift by allowing me to reflect the love I have for him back onto me.

When you come to the return of self-love, you'll feel the liberation of being you. It will no longer feel like anything is wrong or missing. You'll feel content and whole just as you are.

Stop Waiting and Start Living

The best piece of advice I received during separation with my twin flame was to stop waiting and start living. Since I knew we were destined to be together I had put quite a few things on hold in awaiting reunion. Waiting and holding back created a lot of frustration in me. Because I was holding off some aspects of my life, I began to grow impatient. Here's the problem with that; twin flames can feel and sense each other's energy. And by holding onto the energy of impatience, I was unknowingly putting pressure on my twin, which pushed him further away. Thus, in order to release that pressure, I needed to stop waiting for him to come back to me. Everything that I was planning to do when my twin returned I had to do first on my own. To that end I took a tropical vacation, spruced up my apartment, and got a kitten. I had to live fully and not hold anything back from myself.

Here's the truth. If you don't believe that you are worthy of every good thing on your own, how can you expect to be able to receive the goodness of your twin when they're ready for you? You must be ready to receive every good thing now. And you must hold nothing back from yourself in order to then hold nothing back from your twin. God loves you so much that he wants you to have all good things. Start by getting into agreement with God and you'll be surprised at how quickly your twin will start to come around again.

Unusual Situations Reserved for Twin Flames

*A*T THE BEGINNING OF this book, I mentioned that a twin flame relationship was a like a soulmate relationship on steroids. In a nutshell, as you may have experienced and seen, twin flame relationships bring out more of just about everything. In addition to everything being *more*, you will also have experiences that will seem highly unusual and at times unbelievable. In fact, the more unbelievable the experience, the more confirmation you'll have that you are in a twin flame relationship.

Connecting with Your Twin

The major advantage that twin flames have over other romantic relationships is that, pretty much from the beginning, they can connect spiritually. It's not as if spiritual connections don't occur with other relationships. It's that with a twin flame one, one or both are consciously aware that they can. Herein lies the double-edged sword of the twin flame connection. Because your twin is hypersensitive to your thoughts and feelings, they can sense when you're being disingenuous or pushing them away. For example, lying to your twin is simply not an option. They will see right through your lies. Just like biological twins, twin flames can sense when the other is not well or is perhaps having a bad day. The following are examples of connecting with your twin outside of the 3D.

Telepathic Communication

Twin flames have the capacity to communicate nonverbally and even across the miles. Even looking at my twin, we are able to communicate volumes. Your twin will communicate with you in whatever way he or she can. For example, my twin often communicated with me in dreams.

Telepathic Sex

Feeling your twin in the 5D sexually is a way you can feel close to him or her even during separation. The experience of sexual intimacy with your twin in the spiritual realm doesn't always have to mean sex. It can come through an experience of feeling a warm embrace or an increased sensation of heat throughout your body. For me, confirmation of 5D affection from my twin was always accompanied by tears and that's how I knew he was reaching out to me.

Journaling or Talking to Your Twin's Higher Self and Getting Answers

In the beginning I suggested keeping a private journal to your twin. In this journal, you can write letters, poems, songs, or thoughts. I would also suggest not giving it to your twin or sharing it with them unless they are already open to the twin flame concept. You can also share it if you've reached the point where you are both open and vulnerable with each other.

From the moment I experienced conscious integration and ascension of my twin's and my souls, I have been able to communicate openly with my twin's higher self. Through my journaling, I was able to ask my twin flame's higher self about certain things and get answers. At times I just wanted to know what his higher self wanted me to know. And each time I got an answer. One time, however, when we were really close to reunion, I asked my twin's higher self a question that he didn't answer. It didn't matter how many times I asked, the answer never came through. It was then that I realized my twin wanted to communicate some answers in the 3D rather than the 5D.

Manifesting Desires Into Reality

Instant manifestation is a byproduct of the spiritual upgrades you receive as a result of doing your work and also of being in a twin flame connection. The more you surrender to the process of your twin flame journey, the more you'll see magical manifestations happening in your life. God's work is important and he will reward your obedience to his plan by helping you financially. In other words, all of your suffering is not in vain. During the twin flame journey, you will have to make sacrifices. Often twin flames have to let go of jobs, homes, families, and geographical locations in order to come into reunion with their twin. God recognizes these sacrifices and is prepared to compensate you. Therefore, as you surrender and do your spiritual homework, you will see coincidence after coincidence happening to help you along your life path. Doors will begin to open that you couldn't open on your own. The vibrational frequency of unconditional love is a high frequency and is aligned with abundance.

Affirmations & Visualizations

To that end, you must stay in high vibrational frequency with your thoughts. A great way to remain positive is to have a daily practice of affirmations and visualizations. Make a list of things you want to see manifested between you and your twin and then read them out loud into a voice memo app or recorder. Listen to your affirmations daily. When I would find myself becoming negative about our situation or thinking he didn't care, I would listen to my affirmations and feel much better.

Since it takes the same amount of energy to think positively or negatively, why not stay in a positive mindset? If you're writing down affirmations that seem impossible to manifest, then you're doing something right. Affirmations *should* feel weird at first. At first, reading them or listening to them can make you feel like you're just having "wishful thinking." For some it can even feel like you're lying to yourself, since some things you desire about you and your twin can seem so farfetched. But eventually listening to those phrases will start to sound normal. And you might even begin to start believing them. That's when you know your practice is working.

For years I had practiced affirmations and visualizations, so I was quite familiar with how it works. A few months into our separation, I decided to record affirmations about us being in love and getting back together. Often I would listen to these affirmations when I was driving. After a few times of listening, something bizarre happened. Usually with voice memo on an iPhone, you listen to the recording and when it's done, the sound shuts off. But one day as I was driving to work, I was listening to the affirmations and it began playing on loop. Then when I tried to hit stop, it started again by itself. Again I tried to turn it off by turning of the sound system in my car. Mysteriously, it turned back on through the Bluetooth even though the sound system was off. Finally in a panic, I turned off the car and closed the voice memo app on my phone. The app turned back on and began playing the affirmations again through the Bluetooth on my car even though everything was turned off. It was as if my Angels were telling me that I needed to keep on hearing those affirmations so I would believe. Now you might think this was a one-time fluke. But, no! Every subsequent time I listened to my affirmations about my twin, the same thing would happen. In fact, I had to be really careful about when and where I listened to them, because my renegade voice memo app might have made me look crazy if those affirmations had started playing in public. My story *is* crazy. But I believe it's a message about the importance of practicing positive affirmations.

In addition to positive affirmations, I would visualize life with my twin. Every day I would visualize us living together, being married to each other, and communicating superbly together. With each visualization, I would non-verbally invite him in to join me.

Try to keep your visualizations positive too. Many people will visualize scenarios they don't want, such as their twin sleeping with someone else. Only focus on what you want to see manifested and you will bring that which you want into form.

Darker Forces Trying to Keep You and Your

Twin Apart

As nutty as this may sound, the closer you and your twin get to reunion, the more adversity will show up to try and keep you apart. And if your twin flame connection is strong, expect some crap to come your way. People will show up to create chaos and unfortunate circumstances will ensue.

Here's the reality. You and your twin are a powerful couple and an integral part of God's plan to spread unconditional love on the planet. Evil forces don't want unity or unconditional love to reign. I always thought success or failure in romantic relationships was only due to individual choices and behaviors. Well, I believed that until I saw in plain view, the people who showed up to try and keep my twin and me apart. At first it was subtle. It was just a couple of people fabricating stories about me that they told to my twin. Then it started to happen more frequently. Without doing anything wrong I was losing credibility in the eyes of my twin. Finally everything exploded where rumors and invented stories flew around endlessly about he and I. It happened so fast that we couldn't stop to take a breath. The one big question we asked ourselves was, *Where in the world is this coming from?* The way, in which it happened, came completely out of left field. And my twin being the wise person he is answered, "It's the devil."

Now I'm not a crazy religious Bible thumper. But, both he and I have a strong belief in God and Jesus as his son. I never wanted to believe that Satan and his minions had a plan in my story, but it seems to be so. To me, honestly, it just sounded completely nutty. But I would have to say, hats off to my twin on this one. In reality, no other explanation exists. The people who created chaos by starting and perpetuating lies about both he and I, literally came out of nowhere. These workers, on the side of darkness and evil, were trying to create a permanent rift between my twin and me. I have absolutely no doubt about that.

In spite of all of the adversity we endured, here's the kicker...God always wins. In fact, the people put in our path to keep us apart, brought us closer together. Each time one person said one thing about the other or each time an event occurred causing an exaggerated response, we were forced to talk about it. And in talking we grew to know each other better. Through this adversity we learned to problem solve. We also got to know the depth of each other's character. Not knowing him much before, I learned how spiritual my twin is. Having had trust issues probably most of his life, my twin learned that he could trust me. But the best part was that we learned to protect each other. And protecting one another is absolutely essential in a twin flame relationship. Because your mission together is incredibly important to not only humanity, but also the planet, you will encounter more adversity if you're not a united front.

Protect Your Twin and Yourself

The following is going to sound like plain-Jane relationship advice, but it's of top importance when it comes to twin flame relationships. Here it is: *Refrain from complaining about or criticizing your twin flame to other people.* You must uphold their honor. First of all, your twin is hypersensitive to your criticism and will know if you're talking bad about them behind their back. Secondly, saying anything negative about your twin to others is a form of betrayal. Thirdly, when you show others that you and your twin are not a united front, you allow strife to enter your relationship. I repeat; this is probably good advice for any romantic relationship. But remember how I mentioned that darker forces *will* attempt to keep you and your twin apart? When you show weakness in your couple by showing negativity toward your twin in the face of others, darker forces will have a feeding frenzy.

Here is the reality. Even in your state of spiritual enlightenment, you are still human. You're still vulnerable to psychic attack. Furthermore, you're not a perfect human either. When you criticize or complain about your twin, you're attempting to put yourself at a higher level than him or her. In essence you're saying that you're better than them. The truth is, you and your twin are equals. You are woven of the same cloth, so to speak. So neither one of you is higher than the other. You may be at different levels of development in different areas but in the end you are one.

Furthermore, you must spend some time each day putting a shield of protection around your twin. Call upon Archangel Michael to shield you and your twin in white, purple, and blue lights to repel any darker energy. Also you can ask Archangel Michael to clear away any lower energies from both of you. This clearing and protection will ensure that you and your twin are constantly surrounded by light.

Revisiting the Dark Night of the Soul

The clearing process that takes place during the dark night of the soul, which includes crying, mood swings, and even depression will come back when you're ready for reunion. During the process of reuniting with my twin, instead of being elated, I went through another mini dark night of the soul. Remember those days when you would look at his or her picture and break down sobbing? Yes, this does come back briefly. I look at it as a final sweep before guests arrive to a party. When I experienced it, I was baffled that it should come about again. But what I truly felt inside was a sense of relief. It was the realization that all of the suffering I endured wasn't for nothing. After the deep emotions came a sense of gratitude to God for finally allowing my twin and I to be together. I also felt a deep sense of gratitude that I wasn't alone on the journey because I knew then that my twin was experiencing something similar. Up until that point I had thought that he was cool, calm, and collected and that I was a crazy mess. But I learned that he too had been suffering. Perhaps in a different way, but he suffered nonetheless. The second coming of the dark night of the soul was less about releasing and ascending and more about being humbled by the power and awe of almighty God. When you are faced with God's light in all of his glory, you can't help but be emotional. God is so much bigger than you. And when I saw how he brought my twin and I back together, I couldn't have predicted it if I had tried. We literally had to walk through hell in order to find each other again.

Raising the Collective Consciousness

Every twin flame couple that comes back together helps raise the vibration of the world. During the phase of ego death, it can be easy to get angry when you hear stories of other twin flames getting back into union. You might wonder why your story is so difficult. But try not to worry. With every twin flame couple in the collective who unites, you're getting closer to your reunion with your twin. I like to think of it as a zipper effect. Each twin flame couple is like a single set of teeth on the zipper. As one reunites, the next one is sure to as well. But a more scientific example comes from The Hundredth Monkey Phenomenon.

TWIN FLAME ROMANCE

Perhaps you've heard the story of the monkeys on the Island of Koshima in Japan. Starting in 1952, the Japanese monkey was observed in the wild for over 30 years. Scientists provided the monkeys with sweet potatoes dropped in the sand. While the monkeys loved the sweet taste of the potatoes, they didn't like the sandy taste that accompanied them. One young monkey took her potatoes to a nearby stream and started washing them. Then she showed her mother and siblings how to wash the potatoes. For years most of the monkeys washed their sweet potatoes while others still ate the sandy potatoes. Then one day, all the Koshima monkeys were washing potatoes. For some reason, the potato-washing had reached critical mass and became a learned behavior among all the monkeys. What was even more surprising was that the monkeys, on a neighboring island, who had never seen the potato-washing behavior were also washing the potatoes before eating them. The collective consciousness among the Island monkeys had reached a new level and they were somehow communicating the new behavior without direct communication.[1]

When you hear of a twin flame couple reuniting, rejoice and be joyful. That means you are one step closer to reunion with your twin. Each twin flame couple who reunites is paving the way and opening the path for an easier reunion for other twin flame couples. As they remain in unity through unconditional love, they are enlarging the energy field and holding a space in higher consciousness for all twin flames to awaken.

Reunion with Your Twin Flame

You and your twin will come into reunion when all individual learning and growing is done. Look at it as a graduation from high school or college. By reuniting you are graduating to the next level. But just like a high school or college graduate, you are not a finished product. You and your twin are simply moving into the next phase of development. Your learning and growing will now continue together. Instead of "happily ever after," your mantra will become "happily serving God and others." As lightworkers you will be living a life of service. The selfless and unconditional love will only continue as you move through your mission together. For some, it will look like having children and raising a family together, for others it will be about serving in the world at large. For you and your twin, it may include both. However, by this phase in your development you are no longer worried about what your mission is, you simply allow, trust, and walk forward on the path chosen for you.

Many have asked what reunion looks like and feels like. The answer is different for each couple. Regardless of how you come and stay together, your story will be unique and something to celebrate.

In conclusion, it's my hope that I've answered many of your questions about the twin flame romantic journey. I'm convinced that this is the beginning of many valuable conversations with you and all readers. My Angels and guides are urging you to stay in faith and to remain in the present moment always to make sure you're enjoying your path with your twin.

Furthermore, this is not the end of the journey for us and me as your mentor. As of the fall of 2019, I'm still doing private twin flame readings, coaching, and live events called *Twin Flames Unite*. In addition, my YouTube channel will continue to be a resource for twin flames across the globe: https://www.youtube.com/c/MichelleFondinAuthor. And of course, you can learn about healing and the spiritual path by reading or listening to any of my other books.

Wishing you a lifetime of health, hope, happiness, and unconditional love my friend. Stay in faith and peace always, Om shanti, shanti, shanti.

Twin Flame Q & A

*I*N THIS SECTION YOU will find the answers to some common questions I have received during twin flame coaching and on my YouTube channel. While the questions are not comprehensive to the amount of questions you might have in your mind, I hope these answers help demystify the twin flame journey. If you have unanswered questions you can always check out my YouTube live twin flame Q & A on Tuesdays at 6 p.m. Pacific or join a *Twin Flames Unite* live event.

Q: What if I don't believe this whole twin flame thing?

A: So be it. You will believe what you will believe. God gives you the freewill choice to believe in him so it stands to reason that he also gives you the freewill choice to believe anything else. As humans we only tend to accept what we can comprehend or that which is in our field of vision. Most often we have difficulty accepting, that which comes without tangible explanations. And that is where faith comes in. If you choose to have faith, you'll see miracles unfold in this journey. And if you don't choose to have faith, you probably weren't meant to have this experience in its full capacity.

Q: Can I have more than one twin flame?

A: No. The word *twin* means "double" or "two". It doesn't mean, three, four, or five. My understanding in what I channel is that you have one twin flame and you are the other half of that twin in a soul connection. Any other romantic relationship is either a karmic or soulmate one.

Q: Does my twin know that he/she is my twin flame?

A: It depends on where your twin is on their journey to awakening. Your unawakened twin may have a notion of a special connection with you, even though they may not understand the meaning *twin flame*. But please remember that terms and definitions are not important. What's important is that your twin evolves to a point where they know you are a part of their life purpose.

Q: When will my twin stop ghosting me?

A: As painful as it is to have your twin flame ignore your calls, emails, and text messages, look at it not as ghosting but as helping you find your way through healing. Intuitively, your twin knows that he or she is doing you a disservice to continue to communicate with you when you both have a lot of healing to do. When you work on your healing and mind your energetic space, you'll find that your twin will reach out. It may often take several periods of start and stop communication before all healing in separation is complete. But take heart, when your twin does reach out, he or she is reassuring you that they haven't forgotten you. Remember, they are also on their own healing journey too.

Q: What is a "false twin" and does everyone have a false twin?

A: False twins are generally karmic or soulmate connections that help us prepare for the journey with our twin flame. They can come before or during the connection with our twin. In a false twin connection, it energy can feel similar to that of a twin flame and the trajectory can look very much alike. But with a false twin connection, there exists *something,* a feeling that just doesn't jive with you at times. You will have moments where you feel that this person is an intruder in your life without quite understanding why.

Q: As the "awakened" twin, what can I do to help the "unawakened" twin?

A: The one thing you can do to help your "unawakened" twin is to do the work on yourself and your own spiritual development. Other than that, continue to love your twin unconditionally, even if it's from afar. Your unconditional love will penetrate your twin's energy field and that will help them to awaken.

Also, try to remember that if your twin is not aware of your connection, it doesn't mean they are unawakened. It means they are in a different phase of growing and learning. You and your twin's phases of development will never be exactly the same. They may be more advanced than you in some aspects and you might be more advanced in others. I like to equate it to strengths or weaknesses you might have at school. For example, I'm not that good at math but I'm great at writing. If you were to look at my low level of math comprehension, being a math expert yourself, you might believe I'm not that intelligent. But to look at my intelligence from only that point of view would be silly if you were to ignore my other gifts and talents. The same goes for your twin and his or her spiritual gifts.

Q: Do some twin flames never come back together?

A: The answer is complex. Twin flames who incarnate in this lifetime are meant to come back together in reunion. However, God gives us freewill to choose our path. Given our freewill, some will make the choice to abandon the journey. Others will choose to stay in their karmic or soulmate relationships. Yet, as I've written before, nothing is a surprise to God. Therefore, if you choose not to come back into reunion with your twin flame, God already knew what your choice would be.

Q: How do I know if my twin and I will come together romantically?

A: Your intuition will guide you to the answer once you're able to get silent and trust your intuitive messages. For my twin and me, the intent of our connection came through immediately. Right off the bat, God revealed that he and I would be married. But for each twin flame couple it is different. Most twin flame couples will come together romantically. However, what you may have seen with your situation is that it's a complex connection. When in doubt, look within.

Q: I've heard that twin flame couples often have a huge age gap, if we don't does that mean we're not twin flames?

A: No. This is a common misconception. In the twin flame collectivity of the 21st century, a majority of twin flames have an age gap. But not all will. The most common age gap is between eight to twelve years with the divine masculine twin being younger. It is not clear why this is so. But one reason might be to shatter the paradigm that the woman or divine feminine cannot be older than the man to have a healthy connection. One possibility that I explain on my YouTube video entitled, *Your Younger DM Is a Rock Star* (https://youtu.be/u12QVF-pZ88M), is that your amazing divine masculine saw the trials you were going through as a child and young adult and made the decision to come down to help you.

Q: Is there a way to shorten the separation phase or precipitate reunion?

A: Yes. You can jump timelines to one where you and your twin are in reunion but only if you are both ready for it. By getting to a space of unconditional love and staying there and by working on loving yourself, you can reach reunion sooner. However, be mindful that your twin is also working through his or her own work. And the timing that you want may not be the proper timing for them. Meanwhile, stay in the space of love so that you can help precipitate healing for the both of you. Most of all, relax and stay in faith. Divine timing works best when you go with the flow of the universe and not against it.

Glossary

ASCENSION: In the twin flame journey, ascension means moving up to the next spiritual level

CHAKRAS: The energy centers in the body. There are seven main chakras from the base of the spine to the crown of the head.

DF: Divine feminine

DM: Divine masculine

GUNAS: The three fundamental forces of or qualities of nature as outline by the Yoga Sutras of Patanjali. They are *sattva, rajas,* and *tamas.*

KARMA: Action or deed. It is also the principle of causality, in which a person's intent in taking action in the present equals a particular result in the future.

KUNDALINI: Divine feminine energy that lies latent at the base of the spine.

PATANJALI: A sage who lived around the 2nd century BCE in India and is said to be the father of many Sanskrit texts of which the most famous is the Yoga Sutras.

PRAKRUTI: Physical matter

PURUSHA: The cosmic Self (soul), cosmic consciousness, or the universal principle: unbounded universal energy that has not yet taken form into *prakruti.*

RAJAS: Activity, energy, passion, restlessness; one of the three primary qualities of nature in yoga philosophy.

REUNION: In the twin flame journey, the moment at which twin flames reunite after a period of separation in the 3D.

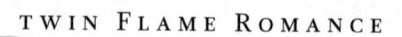

SATTVA: Purity, one of the three primary qualities of nature in yoga philosophy.

TAMAS: Inertia, lethargy, darkness, or dullness, one of the three primary qualities of nature in yoga philosophy.

3D: The third dimension

5D: The fifth dimension

About Michelle S. Fondin

Author, speaker, and YouTuber, has also been a spiritual teacher for over a decade teaching Chopra Center yoga, meditation, and Ayurveda. Michelle has authored over six books including, *The Wheel of Healing with Ayurveda*, *Chakra Healing for Vibrant Energy*, *Help! I Think My Loved One Is an Alcoholic*, and *Enlightened Medicine Your Power to Get Well Now*. She resides in Los Angeles, California. You can learn more about Michelle at fondinwellness.com.

Connect with Michelle on social media:

YouTube: https://www.youtube.com/c/MichelleFondinAuthor
Instagram: @michellesfondin
Twitter: @michellesfondin

Made in the USA
Columbia, SC
18 December 2023